The Object of My Affection

Pinky Tomlin

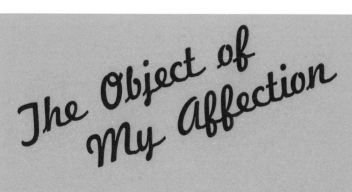

The Object of My Affection

AN AUTOBIOGRAPHY

BY

Pinky TOMLIN

WITH LYNETTE WERT

University of Oklahoma Press: Norman

Library of Congress Cataloging in Publication Data

Tomlin, Pinky, 1908–
  The object of my affection.

  Includes index.
  1. Tomlin, Pinky, 1908– . 2. Singers—United States—Biography. 3. Composers—United States—Biography. I. Title.
ML420.T66A3   784.5'2'00924 [B]   80-5938
ISBN 0-8061-1719-2   AACR2

To my wife, Joanne,
"The Object of My Affection,"
whose life has been blessed with great
compassion, loyalty, and beauty.

Contents

Illustrations

The Object of My Affection

1

Oklahoma, 1933

A hot August wind whistled through the open cab of the Chevrolet truck as I traveled the back roads of southeastern Oklahoma in the summer of 1933. The seat of the gravel truck bounced, making rinky-tink noises, while the dirt roads added an accompanying hum. My summer job, hauling rock at thirty cents an hour, was important to my survival as a hungry young man in his twenties. The two dollars and forty cents I made each day ensured that I'd be able to return to the University of Oklahoma in the fall.

While I was jolting along Bryan County's corduroy roads, my mind was wondering if it was worthwhile returning to law school. I had other ambitions too, and thirty cents an hour didn't seem as if it would propel me far in the musical world. The Depression had a tight hold on everyone's future, whether they wanted to be songwriters, farmers, or lawyers.

While I was mulling my future, a line I'd read in last year's lawbooks popped into my mind. "The object of my affection . . . ," I muttered, and then repeated it twice to the rhythm of the bumpy road and creaky Chevy truck.

The rhyme went no further than that one odd line, though I spent most of the afternoon humming snatches of a melody I worked out to fit it. I knew better than to spend my employer's time thinking about writing music. In 1933 if you were fortunate enough to land a job, you worked tenaciously. Despite the fact that summertime in southeastern Oklahoma seemed desolate and discouraging, this job was vital. It would tide me over until I could return to Norman, Okla-

3

homa, and my school-year job of playing guitar and singing with the campus Boomer Band at the university.

I finished my long day with the line, "The object of my affection," still latched to a corner of my mind. I was glad to get away from that red dust. A day of truck noise, rattling rock, and hundred-degree sun made me look forward to this evening, when a friend and I were going to a party out of town. I'd have to hurry to bathe, pack, and be ready. Glancing in the rear-view mirror as I parked the truck, I saw I was sunburned as usual. The sun and I had never been particular friends because I have a fair, ruddy complexion. As a child, I had a pink tinge to both my skin and hair, and naturally I acquired the nickname "Pinky." I was stuck for life not only with the nickname but with the discouraging tendency to sunburn. A day of driving in the open truck had done nothing to improve my appearance.

I arrived home excited over my plans for the evening. They were really big-time for Depression days. Lynn Abbott, a buddy who actually owned a car, and I were heading for Ponca City, Oklahoma, to see some friends. As I began tossing things toward my "please don't rain" suitcase, my mother came to the doorway of the bedroom and eyed me skeptically.

She questioned me with arms folded primly, "Where are you off to?" She had the firm tone of a concerned mother.

"I'm going to see the object of my affection," I replied breezily, adding my guitar to my baggage. The silly line merely popped into my head. I had no real-life girlfriend to bestow the accolade on at this point. "Yep, the object of my affection."

Mother frowned, obviously having no idea what my scatter-brained remarks meant. Her mind did not run to the frivolous. A woman who had memorized both the Standard and the King James versions of the Bible did not view her gangly, sunburned son's triviality with much laughter. She viewed me suspiciously and then announced, "Not with that complexion!"

She turned and left the doorway. I stood mesmerized, grinning with delight at the obvious rhyme connection. All I had to do now was intertwine "affection" and "complexion." I again hummed the melody I'd worked out while driving the gravel truck, then whistled a

4

few bars as I finished dressing. "Oh, . . . the object of my affection
. . . la, la, la . . . complexion." Heck, I'd work it out on the way to
Ponca City.

All the way north while Lynn drove, I strummed chords on my
guitar and tried various lyrics. When we pulled into the driveway of
the elegant home of Joanne Alcorn in Ponca City, I had my new song
finished. That night I auditioned "The Object of My Affection" for a
roomful of high school and college kids. It was a simple performance,
one tall, pink-haired guy with a guitar. The young people liked it,
graciously telling me that the song was good. Miss Alcorn went out of
her way to compliment me, but I figured that was her job as hostess.

A lot of strange twists of fate occurred that evening. A whole lifetime of relationships began. My song "The Object of My Affection"
went on to become a Hit Parade leader for many weeks. It sold worldwide as records and sheet music for over forty-five years, providing me
a lifetime meal ticket. As for Joanne Alcorn, the young lady who
graciously let me audition the song at her home, she became the true-
life object of my affection. We recently celebrated our forty-second
wedding anniversary.

I'm the first to acknowledge that coincidence and luck intervened
on my behalf through the years, but I like to think that determination
and hard work also played a part. In 1933 I worried that I'd be driving
a gravel truck down dusty roads forever with nothing more to show
for it than thirty cents and a sunburn. But a chance line and some
rambling lyrics altered my course, and music became the all-time
object of my affection.

2

Eros, Arkansas

Music became my life's work, but I was a teen-ager before I had a chance to discover my talents and desires. My early years consisted of the hard times common to most youngsters growing up in the World War I era. Originally my family lived in Arkansas, and, sometime long before then, in England and Ireland. The name Tomlin is derived from Tomlinson, and a family story tells that the original English Tomlinson patriarch had a son who gave him a great deal of trouble. The boy was such a rounder that the father finally shouted, "You're no son of mine!" The succeeding generations dropped the ending and became Tomlin.

The story made good history but didn't impress me as I was growing up a sharecropper's son in the remote hilly terrain of Arkansas. I was born geographically at the real end of the line, near the town of Eros, Arkansas.

It's all right for me to joke about Eros now, for the town dwindled and finally disappeared. We used to say that the best directions for getting to our farm were: "Take the train from Harrison, Arkansas, for about forty miles, then drive by car for another twelve. Switch to horseback for four miles, walk two miles, then swing in by grapevine for the last lap."

Eros was the name of the Greek god of love. Apparently the spirit of mutual attraction wasn't too prevalent in the Arkansas hamlet. The population of the town dropped to zero.

Making a living was everybody's primary concern in rural America in the early days of the twentieth century. For my family, making a living meant just getting by. We raised cotton and enough corn to feed the livestock. We supplied our own milk, butter and eggs, beef, pork, and lamb. Mother saw that her family of three sons was well fed, but she also saw that her children's opportunities were limited to the meager soil of Arkansas if we stayed on the farm. She became the impelling force toward moving us to town.

My mother's maiden name was Louisa Dobbs. She was the stubborn pioneer type of woman who could make up her mind to do a thing and never be dissuaded. She married George Louis Tomlin and gave him three sons—boys that she wanted out of the backwoods. At one point in her crusade to move she announced, "Now listen here, George, I want to live somewhere *on* the map." As her boys began growing up, her greatest ambition was to move to a town with a good school system.

My dad finally agreed. He sold the few things we owned and then gathered the family around him. I was the baby of the family after brothers Walter and Troy, and I was still under school age, but the idea of moving seemed very exciting. I looked up at my father with wide eyes as he said, "Boys, you're gonna get some schoolin'. We're heading for a town."

We chorused, "Where?"

"Durant, Oklahoma."

The words sounded like a foreign land as I tried them out on my four-year-old tongue—a new place, a new town, a new state. It didn't mean too much to me except that I'd get to see my Uncle Dave.

We left Arkansas on the slow night rail coach. Talk about a slow train through the south. We huddled at the station in the twilight, waiting as the creeping engine chugged toward the station. My mother grabbed Walter, Troy, and me against her, holding us protectively. "Don't let them see the bright headlights," she whispered to my father. "They'll be scared and won't get on!"

I struggled away from my mother's embrace, determined to look at the big iron horse that would take us to a new place to live. Even at age four I could sense there wasn't much to leave behind. Eros was a good place to be *from*. I left my birthplace without misgivings, heading west with little more than the clothes on my back and my head of pink hair.

3

Durant, Oklahoma

Durant, Oklahoma, is today a thriving town with light industries such as mattress manufacturing, plastic assembly, and toy and electrical component output. Its farming base is peanuts, cotton, watermelons, and soybeans. Recreational facilities at Lake Texoma and the four-year state university, Southeastern State University, are two of Durant's star attractions. When we moved to Durant in 1913, the town was merely a sleepy crossroads village only six years past being part of Indian Territory.

Durant is in the middle of Choctaw Indian country. Many Indian families had settled in Bryan County after the Five Civilized Tribes' removal from the east in the 1800s. What later was named Bryan County was part of the Choctaw Nation under Doak's Treaty of 1820. The first permanent building was built by Dixon Durant in 1832, and the town of Durant began. On the east the famous Texas Road served travelers. The Missouri, Kansas, and Texas railway, known as the Katy, came through the town, and the old Butterfield Stage route passed southeast of the village.

Durant lies in the crescent along the Red River known as "Little Dixie." In the early 1900s many small-town southern prejudices were ingrained in the town. Negroes were not allowed in the city after dark. Most of the money of the town was concentrated in the hands of a few families. The real power in Durant in the twenties and thirties was held by the town's lawyer and banker. Coincidentally, these men's names were Hatchett and Slaughter. Imagine my mistrust, growing up in a town in which the lawyer was Claude Hatchett and the banker was Bill Slaughter.

8

Believe me, when the Tomlin family arrived in Durant, we made no social splash at all. George, Louisa, and their three boys simply faded into the fabric of small-town life without a notice. My father went to work for his brother, Dave Tomlin, at the dray line.

Dray lines were the moving vans of the era. Wagons with flat tops and removable sideboards and tailgate were pulled by teams of horses or mules. My childhood impressions of the rigs were so vivid I still remember the names of the teams—Lady and Diamond, Bill and John, Dude and Dan, and Bert and Clyde.

Our first home in Durant was across the tracks on the south side. It was not the best part of town, but that was where I started school. As soon as we were financially able to move to the north side, Mother insisted that we change schools. Along with the move to the "good" side of town, Mother upgraded my wardrobe. She decided that my entrance into the new school demanded elegance. Bless her heart, she outfitted me in an outlandish Little Lord Fauntleroy shirt with a broad white Buster Brown collar and a black sash tie folded in front.

In this wild getup I went off for my first day in the new school. As I stood in the hall waiting for the classroom to open, a bulky kid with a tough face walked up. He eyed me with disdain and then announced, "I'm Marvin Moore. Known around here as *Mean* Marvin Moore."

I gulped twice, wishing my mother had not been so ambitious about my clothing. Marvin put out his broad hand and yanked my sash tie. It tore loose like a piece of tissue paper.

I didn't stop to think. I punched at him, poking my fist blindly toward his face. Somehow I connected and caused Mean Marvin a bloody nose. Stunned, he turned and hightailed it down the hall, yelling, "Don't mess with that pink-headed kid!" In one day I acquired a tough reputation, even though I was incredibly skinny, shaking in my shoes, and sporting ridiculous duds.

It would be unfair to call Durant a "tough" town, but the manly art of self-defense seemed a good thing to learn. My brother Troy and my friend Fenton "Duke" Taylor taught me what they knew about physical fitness. Things went easier for me then, and I never wore Little Lord Fauntleroy shirts and ties again.

Later Mean Marvin Moore and I became good friends. He even

asked me to play quarterback on his various football teams. Marvin and Duke went on to star on the University of Oklahoma football team, so I fell into good company early in my career.

The remark about the "pink-headed kid" sealed my fate. I was called Pinky from then on. My parents named me Truman Virgil Tomlin, but, with my sunburned face and pink hair, Pinky was inevitable. All the boys in my family had nicknames. My oldest brother, Walter, was known as "Cotton" because of the enormous amount of white hair that sat on his head like a cotton patch. Troy, who grew to be six feet, four inches tall—most of which was extremely long legs—gained the nickname "High Pockets."

During the years we lived on the north side of Durant, our house was pretty nice for the times. It had a front room, a dining room, a kitchen, a back porch that held the icebox, and two bedrooms for the five of us. One other important aspect was the storm cave. Residents of tornado-prone Oklahoma often called the cellar the "fraidy hole." When not in use as a place of refuge, the cellar served as a cool, dark storage place for potatoes and other vegetables.

Another necessary adjunct to the house was the well. We hauled water for cooking, drinking, and bathing. The well was used as a cooler. A bucket of milk or butter let down into the water stayed nicely chilled and didn't spoil.

We had, of course, an outhouse, a two-holer. Behind that stood a barn, then a fenced-in lot for cows, chickens, two pigs, and my pony. My transportation to and from school was that little horse. He was also my transportation to and from work. On my way to school via pony express I delivered milk. Returning home, I'd stop and collect the empty quart containers and the thin dimes that were payment. Ten cents a quart was the going rate for fresh milk—and, boy, it was fresh. I milked two cows every morning at six, and repeated the procedure every evening. Milking isn't a hard job, but anyone who has ever worked with dairy cows will confirm, you have to *be* there without failure.

After school and work, if there was free time, my brothers and I would play games or retire to the front-porch swing. In the summertime the big swing was a favorite place for catching the evening breeze. The only sport was observing the people and the few cars that passed by.

In the winter we did all our heating with wood. Great log heaps lined the path from the back porch to the outhouse. It was a practical arrangement. Anytime anyone ventured out to the toilet, on his way back he was expected to pick up a few logs and deliver them to the house.

During the first five years we lived in Durant, our home had no indoor plumbing, no electricity, and no gas. Potbellied stoves heated the living and dining rooms. A flattop stove with lifters served the kitchen. Our famous Saturday-night baths featured well-drawn water heated on the flattop stove. The hot water, poured into a tin tub, was used for washing clothes and people.

There was no such thing as a telephone in our life. Before 1920 only a handful of phones existed in all of Bryan County. Conditions by today's standards were roughing it, but the low standard of living simply contributed to my early determination to better my circumstances. By the time I'd completed grammar school, I'd already made up my mind to leave home as soon as possible. During some of the worst stretches I'd remind myself, "Pinky, for your own survival, you *have* to leave here."

Were we really poor in those days? Sure. Wasn't everyone? In Durant almost everyone was poor except the Hatchetts and the Slaughters, yet we were never the demoralized and humiliated poor later portrayed in *The Grapes of Wrath*. After all these years I still resent the jokes told by comedians about conditions and desperation that produced Okies.

My family was not a close one—although not from lack of love. It was from the sheer necessity of everyone working all the time. My brothers and I worked at anything we could find to help make ends meet. Our time for socializing was as limited as our finances. Times were hard, and so was the burden on everyone in my family. Besides the money from my milk route, I held a lot of other jobs during my school years. I shined shoes, bundled and cashiered at the Dixie Store (owned by E. C. Terrel), delivered papers, picked cotton, chopped corn, pulled peanuts, and tended the milk cows. My whole family

11

worked similarly, and the work went on before and after school as well as on weekends and holidays. These considerations made family life almost nonexistent. About the only time we were all together was mealtime. Mother did all the cooking, serving, and cleaning up. Neither my father nor any of the three boys ever thought of helping her.

Mealtime meant my parents at the opposite ends of the table, my older hungry brothers along one side, and me alone on the left. If there was fried chicken, it seemed to go around opposite me. For a long time I was convinced that a chicken had nothing but a neck and wings.

Amusement meant inventing fun that didn't cost money. In Durant there was basically "no place to go." There was also nothing to do but work. As a result we learned to work hard even when we played. We rigged handmade fishing poles, dug worms for bait, and used rocks for hunting. I had a reputation as a good aim. One day my dad handed me four rocks. "Here, Pinky, see what you can come up with in the meadow."

I dropped the stones in my pocket. "Maybe I'll get a rabbit," I said.

"Son," drawled my father in his deep voice, "when I send you out with four rocks, I expect you to come back with four rabbits."

He added a message about a lickin' if I failed entirely. Right away I learned that hunting was more than just fun.

For fishing and swimming we had to walk four miles into the country to Blue River. The stream is spring-fed and runs cold and clear through the low valleys. In the summer we especially appreciated its icy temperature. Many years after the dust bowl, trout were introduced into the cold waters of Blue River and thrived in the swift stream. In our day Blue was known simply as the best spot to find a swimmin' hole.

Along our route to Blue River lay a large watermelon field. It belonged to Mr. Edgerton, a local farmer. It's a known fact that boys, swimming holes, and watermelons are an age-old combination. We made it a habit to swipe a couple of Mr. Edgerton's melons, chill them in the cold river, then have a feast after our swim. Blue River ran so swift that we had to tie a long pole across the river to keep the melons from washing downstream.

One afternoon we'd had a fine time playing in the river. Troy shouted, "Eating time!" Everyone was ready for the melons. As we started diving to retrieve our watermelons, Mr. Edgerton came into view over the hill. There was sudden panic as we struggled to submerge his stolen produce and wiggle the makeshift dam back into place. I grabbed a couple of melons and tried to hold them underwater while keeping my own head above the current. Troy shoved another melon into my slippery hands—three watermelons—I was all gangly arms and legs, gulping and bobbing and trying desperately to keep those three huge melons from bobbing into sight.

The farmer stood on the bank, hands in his overalls pockets. He stood there casually, acting bored while we thrashed about like crazy dervishes. Finally he called to us, "O.K., fellers, don't drown yourselves! Come on out and sit in the shade, and we'll carve up a couple of the best of them melons."

General shouts of rejoicing filled the air. We scrambled out of Blue River with our loot, but Walter put a damper on the party by asking Mr. Edgerton, "Are you going to tell our parents?"

The farmer thought for a moment and then said, "What about a deal? I won't snitch on you young watermelon thieves if you'll take turns guarding my melon patch."

That was the best deal we'd ever heard. We took up our vigilante duties that afternoon and applied ourselves diligently for the rest of the summer. To keep matters fair, however, we charged Mr. Edgerton a watermelon now and then for our services.

We hated to see summer end, but fall brought holidays that were special. Halloween meant trick or treat. In our case, treats were hard to come by and tricks appealed to boys anyway. Turning over outhouses was great traditional sport in small towns. One Halloween my brothers and I were so eager to continue this tradition that we started in our own alley with our own outhouse.

Brother Walter reasoned things this way: "Our brand-new outhouse is liable to be a prime target for mischief-makers."

"Right," agreed Troy. "We better take care of it ourselves."

"Yep," I added, "we ought to save it from *real* troublemakers!"

We snickered gleefully and ran out to the alleyway, shoving the new structure face down into the red clay and weeds. We then continued our rounds, noting when we returned home that our outhouse was back in its upright position. Surprised, we went inside. Father was sitting in his usual chair, looking more stern than necessary, holding a leather strap in his hand. Obviously he knew we were the culprits who'd turned over the outhouse. The trick didn't set well with him—he was occupying the facility at the time. Fortunately Mother stepped in and saved us from his making good use of the leather strap.

4

First Banjo

My musical career began as a form of hero-worship. Once I'd heard Red Roundtree play his banjo, I knew I'd never be the same until I could play the banjo too.

It didn't bother me that I'd never held a banjo and hadn't the faintest idea how to play it. I was determined to get the musical instrument, and then I'd figure out how to play the thing. I scouted all the secondhand stores in Durant. At Mr. Wilson's I found a banjo in fairly presentable condition. I tried to act nonchalant though my fingers were itching to hold it. "Say, Mr. Wilson, how much for that old banjo up on the rack?"

"Six bucks, Pinky."

Six dollars! That was a fortune! "Well, how much would I have to put down to buy it on the installment plan?"

"A dollar down and a dollar a month."

"Sold!" I said and produced the limp dollar bill that I had hoarded. As he handed me the banjo, I saw myself as a potential Red Roundtree launching myself on the way to fame and fortune. My only problem was finding the rest of the money to pay off my instrument.

After I'd paid that first dollar down, I paid another dollar every time Mr. Wilson caught up with me. He finally tired of chasing me and settled for five dollars total.

I now had a banjo but no music. For twenty-five cents I purchased *Guckert's Chord Book*. This put me into the banjo-picking business in a big way. I found that my affinity for the banjo was no mistake. It was easy to play, and I seemed to have rhythm and style. I learned all the chords from Guckert's book and then went on to invent a few combinations of my own. I soon had the reputation of being the best banjo player in the area. This reputation was probably helped by the fact that Durant didn't have too many banjo players in 1923.

It was that banjo that led me to my first professional musical job. I was fifteen. Like most other boys, I spent Saturdays downtown at the square. Durant was on the route of the medicine shows. The Saturdays at the open market were a combination of country fair, garage sale, and carnival. The whole affair went under the title of a medicine show because it was the patent-medicine men making their pitches that dominated the noise. Everyone came to town on Saturday—townsfolk, farmers, Indians, and kids. Many of the local Choctaws still wore braided hair, hairbands, and blankets in those days.

Early Saturday morning Market Square would fill up with farmers displaying cotton, corn, oats, wheat, tomatoes, cucumbers, and beans. A quarter was the selling price for a bushel of potatoes.

Next the drummers would arrive with their sale goods packed in trunks. About the time the crowd reached "selling size," the pitchmen would move in with their patent-medicine spiels. One pitchman came to Market Square every other Saturday, working from the back of his pickup truck. He'd let down the tailgate to form a crude stage, then clap his hands, holler, and start selling.

As the man was getting out of his truck to start his day's work, I walked up, banjo in hand. "Sir, I'd like to work for you," I blurted. I held up my banjo to show what I had to offer.

The man looked at me without interest. He wore a dingy white shirt, black string tie, plaid sport coat, and white-kid shoes. "Ain't selling banjos, sonny."

"No, no, I *play* the banjo," I told him hurriedly. I slicked down my pink hair and dusted my hand across the banjo. "I'll play music and that'll draw a crowd for you. Then you sell 'em *your* stuff."

Apparently I'd struck a chord with the salesman. He appraised me. I stood up stright, grinning and thinking he was checking out my appearance. Next he inspected my banjo. I decided he was checking it for quality. Finally he snapped his fingers, leaned toward me, and inquired, "But how *loud* can you play that thing?"

Deflated, I realized it wasn't talent or showmanship he cared about—it was loudness. Volume was the key to success in his opinion. "All right, how's this for loud?" I asked, and then launched into a finger-breaking, ear-shattering rendition of 1924's most popular song, "Sweet Georgia Brown." I followed that with "Tiger Rag" and "Tiptoe Through the Tulips." When I finished, I curled my hand, trying to restore circulation. I looked at the pitchman expectantly.

"That'll do," he muttered. "Start in fifteen minutes. I'll pay you a buck each time you gather in a big crowd where I can make my pitch."

That afternoon I worked five shows for the medicine man. Five dollars—I'd made back the price of my banjo in one day! It didn't bother me that the pitchman had probably made twenty or thirty dollars from each crowd I'd gathered. Everyone was happy, the salesman, myself, and the people who bought the tonic that cured "anything from pneumonia to snake bite."

In reality, the "medicine" was mostly molasses, strawberry flavoring, and alcohol. The alcohol ran about 25 percent. At a dollar a bottle it was popular, if not particularly effective as a remedy.

You're probably wondering whether my Saturday earnings ended up in poker pots. The answer is "not very often." Money was still too hard to come by to be lost foolishly. By the time I was in my teens, my father was working on a standby basis as a United States marshal's deputy. He made $35 a month, in addition to his regular police salary of $65 a month. The times he was called on to perform as a deputy marshal, he drew $125 a month. But these jobs rarely lasted longer than a month. Times were still hard in the Tomlin household. The extra $5 I made on Saturdays was an essential contribution.

More than the money, however, the early medicine-show stints with my banjo proved how exciting music could be. I discovered I could entertain people with my music. The money was secondary, but it confirmed that I might be able to pay my own way by doing what I liked best. The thought of playing and performing and actually getting paid for it set me dreaming. Again, the future seemed to lie outside Durant. Once I mentioned my ideas to my mother, but she only scoffed, "Oh, Pinky, there you go chasing rainbows again!"

I didn't quit dreaming—and I didn't limit myself to small-town dreams. I had a deep feeling that there really might be gold at the end of my particular musical rainbow.

5

Louis Armstrong

During high school I tried my hand at several forms of making music. I sang in the glee club, played the drums in the band, and, most important to my future career, added the guitar as my second instrument. My timing in learning to play the guitar was perfect. The instrument was beginning to make its way into the jazz world as a percussion instrument. It was simple to transfer my knowledge of chords from banjo to guitar.

My banjo reputation landed me another musical job while I was in high school. A Dixieland band called the Southern Melodians was Durant's resident dance band. The group played at country-club dances and made out-of-town appearances at Ardmore, Hugo, and Atoka, with occasional daring ventures across the state line to play at Denison and Sherman, Texas. The Southern Melodians were always on hand in Durant to open new drugstores or ice-cream parlors.

Bill ("Dusty") Rhodes, business manager for the band, had heard me play the banjo. He'd even hinted I might come around and try out for the banjo spot with the Southern Melodians. A small hint was all I needed. Imagine how impressed I was when my first performance with the group was the Durant County Club—a place I had not visited in any other capacity. My playing was well received and landed me a semipermanent niche with the band. Later I also played guitar with the Southern Melodians.

I enjoyed my work with the small band. I might have gone on playing with them indefinitely if luck had not intervened the summer I was sixteen. I received a telegram that launched me into adventures I'd never dreamed about.

18

Joe Glaser, manager of Louis Armstrong's famous riverboat band, heard about me while he was in Dallas, Texas. Later, when the Armstrong band was planning to play a riverboat stint from Saint Louis to New Orleans, Glaser offered me a job.

Telegrams were rare enough in Durant to cause a stir. Any telegram was news, but a Western Union message to a sixteen-year-old kid was a sensation. The entire town soon knew that the telegram existed and precisely what it said. I was the center of attention, the universal question being, "Hey, Pink! You gonna go?"

"You kidding?" I responded. From the moment I opened the message, I was making plans to land in Saint Louis.

My joyous planning was cut short by my mother. She took a dim view of the job offer. "A boy shouldn't go on a riverboat," she argued.

"Why not? It's a good place to make music."

"It sounds wrong. Sinful!" My mother's Hard-Shell Baptist upbringing was written all over her frowning face.

"Please, Mom, it's only a summer job. I'll be back in a few weeks, and then I'll go back to the Southern Melodians—and church. I can't pass this up. Louis Armstrong!"

She ended our discussion with a curt "I'll talk to your father."

The conference between my parents ended with a united front. We took a family vote, two parents against and one sixteen-year-old boy in favor of the jaunt. I argued, pleaded, whined, and threatened, with no results. My father gave me the silent treatment, paying no attention to my impassioned pleas. My brothers tried to stay neutral, indicating that the whole situation was beyond my reach anyway. The Southern Melodians took a blasé position, showing they weren't too happy about being without a first-chair banjo player for the summer. Dusty Rhodes, the band's manager, became downright angry that I preferred playing on a riverboat with Louis Armstrong to hanging around Durant all summer.

The matter was finally settled when Armstrong's manager, Joe Glaser, sent me a bus ticket to Saint Louis. I didn't need to think twice. If I didn't go now, I'd never leave Durant. I was on the next Trailways bus out of town, bouncing along with my banjo on my knee.

I hadn't been out of Oklahoma except for the jaunts across the Red River with the Southern Melodians to play one-night stands in Texas border towns. Since moving to Durant from Arkansas when I was four, I'd spent my life in one small southeastern Oklahoma town. Now Saint Louis seemed as exciting to me as New York, Paris, or Hong Kong.

When I stepped off the bus in downtown Saint Louis, I stared like the wide-eyed, small-time kid that I was. Yes, I was impressed by the big buildings and bright lights, but it was more a matter of confirmation than awe. I'd always *suspected* there was a big world out there. Joe Glaser was on hand to meet me, and I turned to him, laughing. "Wow! It's a big world after all."

He patted me on the back, took me to a midtown hotel, and asked tactfully, "Need a few dollars expense money in advance?"

Indeed I did. I stretched the money through my entire first week, eating mostly doughnuts, coffee, and cheese sandwiches. Most nights I stayed awake listening to the sounds of the city. They were real music to my ears. Again, I decided to dream big. Surely there were places I could parlay my musical ability into chances for money and adventure.

During the first week we rehearsed daily. When I first went to meet Louis Armstrong, I was tense as an Oklahoma jackrabbit. The rehearsal hall was a small nightclub in the downtown section of Saint Louis. When I walked in, I saw immediately that I was going to be a real standout—the only pink-haired kid in the band. I introduced myself nervously saying, "Hello, Mr. Armstrong."

"Well, hi-ya Pinky," responded Armstrong, giving me his famous warm smile that showed those enormous white teeth. After we'd gone through a light rehearsal, he gave me another smile of approval. Then he gestured casually, including me in his wave, and said, "Boys, let's head on down to the riverboat."

I nearly burst out laughing I was so happy. When we reached the Mississippi River, I was astounded. It lay wide and golden, more than a mile across. Again I had the feeling that this trip was the start of something big.

Stepping aboard the riverboat was a major turning point for me. It confirmed what my inner self had told me for years—that music was the thing for me to pursue and that Durant was not the place to pursue this goal.

Another important aspect of my summer on the riverboat was the tremendous musical education that I received from Armstrong. His distinctive musical styling taught me the intricacies of jazz. I was lucky to meet such a master of the art at a time when I was musically impressionable.

Jazz wasn't new to America in the 1920s, but the musical form had not yet gained the popularity that later took Armstrong on triumphal tours of the United States, Europe, and Russia. At that time jazz bands were usually small bands consisting of five to eight instruments. Most jazz groups were built around individual talents such as Armstrong and his trumpet. Other famous ensembles were formed around Jack Teagarden and his trombone, Earl ("Fatha") Hines and his piano, Coleman Hawkins and his saxophone, and Benny Goodman and his clarinet. Jazz is supposed to have originated in New Orleans, though Chicago sometimes claims to have invented it. It's my opinion that this distinctively American form of band music began in New Orleans, and then was exploited, financed, and exported by Chicago.

In the early days King Oliver reigned over jazz, launching many great careers in Chicago, including Louis Armstrong's. In later years Armstrong's bands became the larger "swing" bands, using several sections with four or five sax players, three trumpets, three trombones, piano, drums, bass, and guitar. When Louis Armstrong was asked to define "swing" music, he said simply, "Why, that's the way everything should be played."

My summer on the riverboat went much too fast. I took in the scenery and the music in great gulps, as if it were all a feast and I'd face famine later.

True enough, when the trip ended and I went home to Durant, no one was much interested in hearing of my musical adventures. The Southern Melodians let me talk but sort of clucked among themselves

21

as if it were no big deal. Were they jealous, perhaps? Or maybe they were only cutting a kid back down to Little Dixie size. It didn't matter to me. I'd been out into a larger musical world. I'd been able to hold my own. From now on, I knew that Durant would never hold me.

6
Oklahoma University

The year 1929 was not an auspicious time for a young man to think of a university education. Herbert Hoover was president of a country heading downhill into a monstrous depression. In the previous ten years there'd been 825 national bank failures, yet through this time families went right on scrimping and saving so children could have a college education. People went right on *singing*, too—a fact that I noted as I attempted to juggle school, money, and music into some self-sustaining combination.

The big songs of 1929 inclued "When It's Springtime in the Rockies," "Star Dust," and "You Do Something to Me." People were humming "Wedding Bells Are Breaking Up That Old Gang of Mine" and listening to a new radio show, "Amos 'n Andy." In 1929 people still looked up when airliners passed overhead. They read with satisfaction that Al Capone had landed in prison. They smiled with pride when construction began on the Empire State Building in New York City. The hit Broadway show was *Fifty Million Frenchmen*, by Cole Porter. In Hollywood, the Academy Award went to *Broadway Melody*. It seemed music was definitely on people's minds.

Back in Durant, however, things went on in the same way. Anyone who wanted to go to college had to find a way to do it on his own. I had the desire for a university education but no financial resources. I figured I'd need luck, talent, and timing. I rated my talent for banjo and guitar as pluses, and I would even sing if necessary. But my timing was wrong. I had no way to support myself at the university in Norman, Oklahoma. I bided my time impatiently, working in Durant and attending Southeastern State College.

23

I finally got my chance. An opening for a guitar player occurred with the campus Boomer Band in Norman. My timing, talent, and determination came together in the fall of 1929. I ignored the Depression and staked out a hitchhiker's spot on Highway 70 outside Durant. My college wardrobe consisted of the one suit that I owned, the pair of pajamas that my mother had sewed, plus two pairs of socks and one set of underwear. All this was either on my back or packed in my "please don't rain" suitcase. I knew that part of my college career would consist of doing my laundry every night so that I'd have clean clothes for the next day.

Arriving in Norman, I was immediately impressed by the size and magnificence of the University of Oklahoma. The huge red-brick library and administration buildings looked out onto the green, grassy ovals filled with beds of red cannas. Owen Stadium dominated the south half of the campus. I counted the number of buildings on campus—thirty-one—more than I'd ever imagined in one educational complex. I was also thrilled by the beautiful two- and three-story fraternity and sorority houses surrounding the campus. There were perhaps twenty houses in all, many built in southern architectural style with large balconies and enormous white columns.

My own accommodations were not as luxurious. At first I settled in at the Golden Hatchett Boarding House on Asp Avenue near the campus. From this place I could walk to class and back to Campus Corner, where I worked at Fred Switzer's Varsity Shop. I was hired to sing three times a day in return for a $7.50-a-week meal ticket. In 1929, that exchange for groceries went a long way. In my hungry opinion it was a marvelous swap—crooning for food. I found I could eat well and have enough left over for an occasional Coke date and a pack of cigarettes. The business arrangement was that I would sing three times a day, accompanied on the piano by Claude Kennedy.

Fred's Varsity Shop catered to students who didn't belong to the fraternities. They used the establishment as a place to go on dates, to eat, or to hear the music. Fred Switzer's friendship was worth millions; he'd cash our checks, then hold them until we gave him the OK that they'd clear the bank. This unique process allowed us to get cash in a hurry to impress a date.

Boomer Band, about 1930, on the front porch of the Sigma Nu House. *Top row, left to right:* Eugene Kendall, trombone, vocal; Byron ("Mick") McFall, bass violin, vocal; Pinky Tomlin, guitar, vocal; Jimmy Godlove, drums; and Ralph Wright, trumpet. *Botton row:* Chester ("Chet") Stinnett, saxophone, vocal; Claude ("Whitey") Whiteman, trumpet; Claude ("Stokes") Kennedy, piano, arrangements; Everett ("Red") Goins, saxophone, vocal; and Johnny ("Junior") Railey, saxophone.

My favorite source of recreation in those early months was the campus theater. The price for a first-run movie, short subject, and newsreel was fifteen cents until six in the evening, a quarter afterwards. Going to the movies was the one luxury I permitted myself. I just had time in the afternoons to finish class, make the fifteen-cent movie, and arrive at Fred's Varsity Shop in time to sing. I'm certain I saw every movie that played Campus Theatre. My favorites were the Bing Crosby musicals. Part of the attraction, of course, was the music, but part was Bing's delightful costar, Mary Brian. I developed a real crush on Mary Brian, telling myself, "If I ever get to Hollywood, that's one girl I'm sure going to look up."

Movies weren't the only thing low-priced in 1929–30. The Blue Plate Special Dinner cost thirty-five cents and consisted of soup, salad, meat, vegetables, rolls, dessert, and coffee or milk. Taxicab rides cost a dime, and for that price you could go anywhere in Norman.

Sociologists later wrote treatises about the Depression, claiming that the poverty created a sense of unity among the people. Perhaps, but I think that the students at the university felt close to each other in those days anyway. Almost all of us were in school because of great determination and willingness to bear personal hardship, but the sense of closeness came from physical reasons also. This was the dustbowl era. We all went about with handkerchiefs over our faces during dust storms, venturing out carefully to dart from class building to residence. Another unifying force was the no-cars rule. The only people permitted to drive on campus were the few commuters from outlying towns. The no-cars rule didn't trouble most of us. Very few students owned cars in the early 1930s. As a matter of fact, a lot of our parents didn't own cars either.

Occasionally, when feeling affluent, we'd shuck out a hard-earned dime for a cab ride in Norman. The rest of the time we walked—to class, to social events, to athletic contests, to dates' residences, to Campus Corner, to the post office, and to downtown stores. The campus was a continual scene of people walking. It seemed everyone passed about twice a day, making for a first-name basis among the enrollment of five thousand. The huge campus sprawled over hundreds of acres, so we had plenty of room to walk. Perhaps this walking led to closer friendships. I know that for some reason I remain closer to college friends than to those I made later, and my affinity for the university remains strong after half a century.

Before arriving at the university, I had decided to major in music. I hadn't considered much beyond that. When it came time to declare a minor, I sort of shrugged and thought it might be nice to study geology since the university already had a worldwide reputation in that field. It was an odd combination, music and geology, but it suited me fine. I figured the prospects for both musicians and geologists were equally risky, yet both held great potential. In a way both geology and music require personal gambles. You have to put your ability and reputation on the line. These qualities I had in abundance—the ability to work hard and the willingness to take chances when necessary.

Majoring in music brought me formal training in theory, harmony, conducting, composing, and voice. All these courses were offered in the School of Fine Arts at minimal fees. The singing I did three times a day at Campus Corner was entirely different from the voice lessons I took in Holmberg Hall. Down at the Varsity Shop I sang such popular tunes as "Star Dust," "Smoke Gets in Your Eyes," "Dancing in the Dark," and "Sweet and Lovely." Professor William George Schmidt, my voice teacher, favored operatic arias as training. Fortunately the professor realized I didn't have that big a voice.

My voice range was that of a second tenor or medium baritone, but the formal training taught me things that are important whether singing grand opera or in the shower. I learned voice placement, breathing, and intonation and had ear training. Though I sang "naturally"—had inherent good pitch and tune—I continued to take singing lessons for many years. The Boy Scouts had something good with the advice, "Be Prepared."

Professor Schmidt heard that I had written a song that was receiving widespread acceptance in the college community. He asked me to bring my guitar to my next voice lesson and perform my composition. After listening to "Object," he scratched his head and decided, "It's pretty poor music, but pretty good jazz."

Not long afterward Professor Schmidt retired. By then my song had won a worldwide following. When an Oklahoma City paper interviewed Schmidt, he kindly said, "I guess it was about time for me to retire as my judgment about the musicality of Pinky's song was dead wrong—as well as my opinion of his ability to perform it."

Some professional musicians have egos that demand they degrade the idea of formal music training. They proudly announce, "Nope, can't read a note." On the other hand, there are a lot of musicians in the popular field who could hold their own in any symphonic orchestra in the land. I fall somewhere in the middle. I sang in the high school glee club, with the Boomer Dance Band, on Campus Corner with piano accompaniment, in films, on records, in person at major theaters, and in Las Vegas. I'd say natural ability for music is the primary requirement for such success, but formal training certainly doesn't hurt.

To my amazement I found that the college community was thriving during the midst of the Depression. I managed to earn $150 a month. That was far more than I could have made "outside." No one supposedly had a lot of money, yet there were at least two expensive fraternity dances each week. These involved tuxedoes, evening gowns, chaperones, corsages, taxis, and other expenses. My excellent job with the Boomer Band allowed me to join the Delta Tau Delta fraternity in 1929.

The Boomers weren't the only band in Norman, but we were the most popular. Our name came from one of the university spirit songs about the Oklahoma Sooners that goes, "Boomer Sooner, O.K.U.!" The Boomer Band had ten members. I was bandleader, singer, and guitar player. Claude Kennedy played piano for the band, as well as accompanying me at other performances. Our brass section was Grady Watts, Claude ("Otts") Whiteman on trumpet, and Gene Kendall on trombone. Johnnie Railey, Chester Stinnett, and Everett Goins made up the saxophone section. Richard Ellegood played bass horn. At various times we had Jimmy Godlove and Bobby Randolph on drums. Byron McFall (later Judge McFall) served as band manager and also played violin and bass horn.

My time with the Boomers was the beginning of the "sweet" music era. Romantic popular songs included "Temptation," "I'm in the Mood for Love," "Love in Bloom," and "I Surrender, Dear." A particularly marvelous tearjerker was "I'm Just a Prisoner of Love."

We performed all the current hits at proms, serenades, and other events. Some songs stayed popular for years, especially if associated with a particular artist. "Love in Bloom" was Jack Benny's theme song. Bing Crosby's signature song was "When the Blue of the Night Meets the Gold of the Day," and Kate Smith's was "When the Moon Comes over the Mountain." These songs proved how a theme song could work to a performer's advantage. I took note of these identity songs, thinking I might try my hand at composing someday.

The Boomer Band's typical date might include a prom followed by a serenade. The fraternity serenade would come at the end of the evening with the band hiring a truck to move over to the sorority house. Fifty or sixty fraternity men would troop along on foot, adding their glee club and special musical talents. Our band could perform almost any type of music despite our basic makeup as a ten-piece Dixieland group. We'd do sweet, jump, jazz, or exotic material as the occasion demanded. We'd even wear funny hats and provide entertainment gimmicks if our employer and audience wanted them.

One gimmick landed me in big trouble. A popular song of the era began "Under a blanket of blue, just you and I beneath the stars. . . ." This romantic ballad was popular with the coeds and was often requested at serenades. One night, however, I belted out a parody, yelling through my megaphone, "Under a blanket with you, we couldn't care less about the stars . . . !" Little did I realize that the dean of women, Edna McDaniel, was spending the night at the sorority house.

The following morning, bright and early, I received a summons from the dean of men. I knew he wanted to discuss my risqué rendition of the ballad. My mind was full of apologies and excuses, tempered by the fact that the parody had gone over great with the audience. On my way to the dean's office I remembered an earlier meeting he and I had had. In the spring the Boomers had played at an

29

educators' convention at the Norman Country Club. During inter-mission one of my compatriots suggested that we go down to the men's locker room for a little nip of bootleg whisky. I was agreeable. The rotgut garbage in the flasks during Prohibition usually cost a dollar a pint, and we foolishly drank the stuff, guzzling greedily for fear of getting caught—and for fear of not getting another chance at the bottle.

I'm certain that many people have the same memories of Prohibi-tion as I do, including the ironic sight of seeing more people drunk than before it became law—or after repeal. In any event, I accepted the invitation to have a drink in the locker room. When we entered, who should be standing next to me, bottle in hand, but the univer-sity's dean of men.

I remembered the incident clearly as I prepared to meet the man again. As I entered his office, it was apparent that his memory was working too. He grinned at me like an old comrade in arms. "Up to your usual antics I see, Pinky."

"Yes, sir."

"Keep it clean, son."

"Yes, sir."

No mention of locker rooms, illegal pints in hip pockets, or my future as a student or musician. Nevertheless, I dropped that particu-lar parody from my act—except by special request.

Actually I had my hands full without going out of my way to antag-onize the deans. Almost all my energy was consumed in carrying a full sixteen-unit course load plus working two musical jobs. We played dance dates every Friday and Saturday night, sometimes finishing well after two in the morning. I was on call to sing at the Varsity Shop three times a day, five days a week. Most days I literally ran from class to work to class to bed. I had come to the university determined to get a good education. I took my course work seriously and maintained a good grade average while keeping my financial head above water.

Summers were a different story. Finding a summer job was almost impossible during the Depression. Full-time jobs for grown men were nonexistent, and that meant that temporary work for college boys was certainly out of the question. Collegians were generally disdained as not knowing how to work anyway. The common derogatory term for us was "jelly beans."

In the summer of 1931 I had a run-in with the proprietor of Swinney's Drugstore in Durant. I begged for a job, pleading, "Mr. Swinney, I really need this summer's work. I'll jerk sodas, scrub the floors, do the stockroom, anything."

"Aw, you college jelly beans are all alike," snorted Swinney. "You're a bunch of soft guys that haven't the slightest idea what work is."

I gathered from his remarks that I wouldn't get the job. He'd riled me up, doubting my ability to work. Second, he'd impugned my college work, which I saw as my ticket to better times. I boasted grandly, "You remember what you said, Mr. Swinney. Someday I'll come back to this small town in a car so big I won't be able to make a U-turn on Main Street. I'll have to drive clear around the block just to park in front of your drugstore. Then I'll lean on the horn until you come out and give me curb service."

I stalked out of Swinney's Drug hot under the collar, aware that my threats were mostly sass and vinegar. The only part that rang true was that I intended to keep my ambitions high. During the Depression there seemed no point in bothering to dream small. True, I was a college jelly bean at the moment, but I didn't intend to remain in that status of having a thousand dreams and no dollars.

I spent my summers driving a truck and had to use my influence with the town lawyer, Mr. Hatchett, to get that thirty-cent-an-hour plum. All during the hot months when I was bouncing and sweating across Bryan County's rough roads, I was eager to get back to Norman and my $150 a month as the Boomer bandleader.

As graduation time from Oklahoma University drew near, I panicked. There was no secure musical future awaiting me. Job offers for people with minors in geology were nil. As far as I could see, I had no future at all in Durant. The Boomer Band was by far the best thing that I'd happened onto. I certainly hated to part company with them, but it seemed that if I picked up my diploma I'd also lose my job.

I was well aware that 1932 was no time to hit the streets looking for

31

a job with credentials in music and geology. Nationally the unemployment rolls topped thirteen million. Oklahoma was in the midst of the great westward migration. Wisconsin had passed an unemployment-compensation law, but no other states were that progressive. Statistics showed that the average farmer earned $341 a year after expenses, about half the sum that he'd made in the 1920s. The hit song of 1932 was the prophetic and plaintive "Brother, Can You Spare a Dime?"

Exciting things were happening, but they seemed far off and unreal. Michigan reigned as collegiate football champion under coach Harry Kipke. *Grand Hotel* won the movie award of the year, while the first drive-in theater opened in Camden, New Jersey. The public also gots its first taste of a federal gasoline tax that year. I wasn't bothered. I still didn't own a jalopy. In Norman, I spent most of my time worrying about the end of my college career.

One morning I had the answer—brilliant, simple, and right under my nose. I'd keep going to school. I ran to the Administration Building and gathered bulletins for all the graduate schools. I'd study anything to stay around and keep my job with the Boomer Band.

After perusing the graduate catalogs, I decided on law school. That settled my future for a couple of years at least.

During the next year my mind attempted to juggle popular song titles with such courses as "Contracts, Real Property, and Torts." One afternoon as I sat propped in Bizzell Library with a large law book in front of me, an unusual case title stuck in my mind. "The object of my affection," I read, thinking that the words had a catchy, internal rhyme to them. I then went on with my studying and thought no more about the line.

It must have lodged somewhere in the back of my mind, for the following summer when I was bumping along southeastern Oklahoma's back roads, the words popped into my consciousness again. Less than six hours later, after my mother's innocent remark about my sunburned complexion, I had a completed song entitled "The Object of My Affection."

After performing the song for the first time in Ponca City, Oklahoma, I reworked the lyrics and melody several times. At one point I used "There are many girls who can thrill me / and some who can chill me, / but I'll just hang around / and keep acting like a clown / until she says she's mine." Later I changed this to "There are many girls who can thrill me / and some who can fill me / with dreams of happiness, / but I know I'll never rest / until she says she's mine."

There was also a verse to "The Object of My Affection" that was carefully planned, telling, ". . . According to definition, / affection is a thing / that seems to change you from the start, / and complexion is a thing, / if affection is to blame, / which will act just like a mirror to your heart . . . / oh . . . / the object of my affection . . . ." (© 1934 Irving Berlin Music Co.; Bourne Music Co.)

In the fall of 1934, when I was back in law school, I worked out an orchestration with Claude Kennedy, the pianist for the Boomer Band. We played the song at various dances, always getting a nice response. "Object" became a favorite at proms and serenades. I'd use a big megaphone to sing the lyrics, and, with the orchestra to back me and a couple of beers to encourage me, the song sounded great. Of course my audience was college students, not music critics, but the occasional adults who served as party chaperones seemed to like it also. It became a popular request at formal tag dances, when a guy had to maneuver carefully to dance with his special girl. Fellows would come up to the bandstand and ask me to give them a signal when the band was about to play "Object." Usually the song was scheduled for just before intermission. A lot of the guys had latched onto the possibilities of being with the object of their affection during that time.

The acceptance of the song in a college atmosphere seemed a good omen to me. I decided to set my sights a little higher. What ways were there to exploit the music? Sheet-music publication? Recording?

I had one resource, Grady Watts, a trumpet player who had been with the Boomer Band several years and had then moved on to play with Glen Gray's Casa Loma Orchestra. Grady was living in Chicago, where the Glen Gray organization did coast-to-coast radio shows and made recordings. I convinced myself that if I could only get to Chicago and look him up the world would immediately sit up and take notice of my song.

In the spring I worked up my nerve to borrow fifty dollars from

Boomer saxophone player Johnnie Railey. I told him, "I've got to make a quick trip to Chicago."

"You'll miss school," he pointed out.

"Not much," I promised. "When I say a quick trip, that's just what I mean."

He loaned me the money. I caught the Santa Fe Chief and sat up in a chair car for the nineteen-hour trip. A visit to the dining car was out of the question. I hit Chicago like an Oklahoma whirlwind, only to be met by the equal resistance of the windy city. My fifty dollars vanished fast. I knew one other musician in Chicago besides Grady, another former Boomer member, Claude ("Otts") Whiteman. Claude took me in, let me bunk in his apartment, and bankrolled me a few candy bars and cheese and crackers.

I didn't care about eating. I was desperate to make contact with Grady, still firmly believing that it was only a matter of time before "Object" would be Chicago's newest tune.

Grady was polite to me in every way when I called him, but he was fairly new to the Glen Gray organization and not in a position to pull much leverage for me. "Come down to the studio," he offered. "Maybe I can at least introduce you around."

I showed up and met Pee Wee Hunt and other members of the Casa Loma orchestra. All seemed pleasant but not particularly interested in my song. I begged Grady time and again, "Listen, buddy, if you can just get Glen Gray's group to record this song and plug it on their radio shows, I'll give you half interest in the royalties."

"Pinky, you know I can't get involved in such a speculative venture. Besides, that's a mighty strange title you've hung on the song. Casa Loma hardly ever does novelty stuff. But listen, I'm glad you looked me up while you were in Chicago."

I realize that there is no tactful way to puncture a fellow human being's dream. But standing in the rehearsal hall in Chicago, I felt my whole life had come to a standstill simply because Grady wasn't in a position to help me peddle "Object."

Back on the Santa Fe Chief, I sang the blues all the way to Oklahoma. If I could somehow have seen into the future, I would have known how lucky I was in not being able to give away a half interest in the song.

When I returned to Norman, the only thing that brightened my spirits was seeing again the young lady from Ponca City who had let me launch "Object" at her house. Joanne Alcorn was now a freshman at the university after winning the Miss Oklahoma title the previous summer. She was seventeen, a Pi Beta Phi pledge, and about the prettiest young girl I'd ever seen. I considered her much too young for me. At one of the proms the Boomer Band played, I sang "Object" as she smiled and winked at me. I smiled back warmly but spoke to her sternly. "Go away pretty brown-eyed baby and see me when you grow up."

After that we saw each other occasionally on campus and even had a couple of rather shy Coke dates. My need to work full time and remain in law school kept my social life at a minimum. I simply couldn't afford the luxury of courting *anyone*. I bided my time, but secretly I felt that one day I might let Miss Alcorn know she was the object of my affection. On one of our casual dates I told her that, because she was one of the first people ever to hear the song, I'd dedicate it to her. That was as brave as I managed to be.

My life was complicated further in the winter of 1934 when my father passed away. He died suddenly of pneumonia before I had time to make it home to Durant. The most vivid recollection I have of this sad time was when I found it necessary to walk into the Durant National Bank and ask for a fifty-dollar funeral loan. There was no savings account from my father's meager salary. The insurance was not even sufficient to meet the funeral expenses. I made the trip to the bank and asked for the fifty dollars.

The president was a distinguished middle-aged man who understood banking well. He was not as well informed about the compassionate needs of fellow human beings. He asked me point-blank, "What do you have for collateral? We never make loans without collateral."

"About all I have is my guitar, a little talent, and the honest intention of repaying you."

"No collateral, no loan."

I left without the much needed fifty dollars.

Somehow my mother, brothers, and I stretched to make ends meet. Mother readjusted to her life as a widow. I went back to law school, but I felt new distress at the limited opportunities in my hometown. Norman didn't seem much more open. I couldn't stay in school and play with the Boomer Band indefinitely. No golden musical opportunities had presented themselves to me. I was going to have to go in search of them.

As the spring of 1934 budded, I did some hard thinking. My heart was set on a career of composing and singing, but I still had to eat.

By chance, one of my law professors had some effect on my decision. He held forth in the dullest of all law courses, "Legal Bibliography." To make matters insufferable, this required class met on Saturday mornings at nine. I barely dragged in most Saturdays after playing with the dance band until nearly three the night before. Most weekends I sat in class yawning and nodding.

On a spring Saturday when the air had turned deliciously warm, the inevitable happened, and I fell sound asleep. My elbow slipped off the desk, my head bobbed, my arm plunged to the floor. As I hit the wooden floor, I jolted enough to break my fall by bracing my whole six-foot, one-inch frame against my outstretched palm. Looking ridiculous as a leaning tower, I attempted to push myself gently back into a seated position.

The only alert mind in that early morning class belonged to the professor. He smiled politely at my predicament and asked, "Mr. Tomlin, would you stay a moment after class?"

I stifled another yawn and nodded agreement.

After class he chided me, with good reason, about my conflicting aims. "You need to work full time, you want to be a musician, and here you are trying to carry a full schedule of law classes. You'll have to reach a decision—a firm one—soon. Do you want to practice law or the guitar?"

Music or law? There was no real question which one I preferred. I replied, "When I add up all the scores on the subjects, the total is music."

"Then the object of your endeavors should be to play with the Boomer Band instead of sleeping through 'Legal Bibliography'."

He'd hit one nail on the head but missed the other. "I realize I can't sleep through law school. But playing frat parties in Norman isn't what I want for the rest of my life, either."

"Don't you know anyone in New York in theater? Anyone in the record business? How about California?"

I shook my head no on all counts, and then I remembered an incident from the year before and commented, "I know one guy in Los Angeles—sort of—Jimmy Grier is a bandleader."

"'Sort of' know him?" questioned the professor. "Do you know him or not?" Law professors don't go in much for generalizations.

"I met Grier via the banking crisis of last year. Remember when so many banks were failing that all the banks closed for a couple of weeks? Jimmy Grier and his orchestra happened to be playing one-night stands through the South. He was stranded in Oklahoma City, all his concert dates canceled, and no way to get back to the West Coast."

The professor looked interested about where this story was leading, both musically and legally.

I explained, "I'd helped book Grier on some of those dates. So tl e Boomers and I brought Jimmy's whole outfit down to Norman. W: put them up for a few days at the frat houses, fed them, got their laundry done, and pooled our resources to tide them over."

"I'm sure Mr. Grier was appreciative."

"Of course. He even made an offhand remark: 'Pinky, if you ever make it to California, be sure and look me up.'" I smiled to myself and then acknowledged, "That's pretty thin air to hang my hopes on."

"I've seen law cases built on less," smiled the professor, apparently thinking that the possibilities were no thinner than turning me into a lawyer. "And I know people do seem to get breaks in California. There's radio, records, and movies. Why, I remember Bing Crosby was only a touring vaudeville act with Harry Barris and Al Rinker until he won the chance to sing with Paul Whiteman's outfit. And why did Horace Greeley insist that young men should head west?"

37

Suddenly I came wide awake. If my professor thought I could do it, why shouldn't I at least try it? I left the law building feeling more excited and awake than I had all semester. I whistled a few lines of "California, Here I Come," then added softly, "Yeah, here I come, ready or not."

7

Good-bye, Oklahoma

"Ten cents a dance, ten cents a dance, step right up and get your tickets now." I heard those lines in my sleep for years after spending the summer of 1934 playing the Lake Kemp resort near Wichita Falls, Texas. The Boomers had been booked into the summer date, and it had to be met before I could think of heading for California.

"Ten cents a dance" was actually a misnomer. The dime ticket entitled the holder to dance three numbers. That was called a set, and after the set floor attendants would remove everyone from the dance floor. It cost another ten-cent ticket to get back on. "The Object of My Affection" became an immediate favorite of the crowd. The men would always buy tickets when they knew "Object" was to be included in the set. This encouraging response to my song kept me plotting ways to make it to the West Coast. But I wasn't saving much money during the Lake Kemp engagement. We made fifty dollars a week plus room and board at the Holt Hotel.

Job-hunting prospects weren't improved for anyone in 1934. Drought and depressed agriculture plagued Oklahoma, Texas, Kansas, and Arkansas, sending droves of dispossessed and dispirited farmers to California. The malicious tag "Okie" was attached to all these unfortunate families no matter what their home state. Okie jokes were both popular and cruel. A comedian got a lot of mileage out of a line such as, "Do you know the definition of a rich Okie?"

"No," the straight man replied. "What is it?"

"An Okie with four mattresses on top of his jalopy."

The humor in that kind of joke was both punishing and derogatory.

The common remark, "The Okies took California without firing a shot," held a lot of humiliation. During this time the only compliment to the wave of immigrants came from Donald Douglas, president of Douglas Aircraft. He said that the Oklahomans were the only people working in his plant who did a day and half's work for a day's pay.

Okies were willing to work—given the chance. In 1934 the nation had sixteen million people on relief. The dollar's value was barely holding at fifty-nine cents. In Germany, Hitler had come to power following the death of President von Hindenburg. Scare tactics were in the headlines internationally, while in America we read of running gun battles between gangsters and the FBI. Alcatraz became a federal prison. A million United Textile workers went on strike. And I had the gall to think I'd take California by storm with one song in my pocket.

There were some good things about 1934, though. Shirley Temple became the nation's dimpled darling. Streamlined trains with diesel engines made transcontinental travel economical and fast. Brothers Dizzy and Daffy Dean pitched baseballs for the St. Louis Cardinals and chalked up forty-five wins between them. In music Cole Porter brought the crowds to Broadway with his hit *Anything Goes*. Popular songs of 1934 included "Deep Purple," "Moonglow," "Winter Wonderland," and "Isle of Capri." I hoped to make it to the West Coast and add "The Object of My Affection" to that list of hits.

Looking back, I wonder why I was so optimistic. Breadlines were everywhere. There were no jobs, with or without a college degree. Perhaps that was just as well. If I'd had security instead of merely a song in my pocket, I might never have parted company with the Boomer Band. As it was, when the summer was over, we separated permanently.

My first stint of traveling took me home to Durant to say good-bye to my mother. While I was there the local paper, the *Durant Daily Democrat*, carried this one sentence on its back page: "Truman Tomlin has a reported agreement to sing with Jimmy Grier's orchestra in California."

It was obvious how important the paper considered this news item.

The story was sandwiched between a column of "Hogs for Sale" and the fascinating notice "A new calf was born at the Taylor Farm."

I couldn't complain, however. The editor of the *Daily Democrat* had been generous in suggesting even a "reported" agreement with Grier. There was no job waiting for me in California. The whole idea of singing with Jimmy's band was wishful thinking. Naturally I intended to look him up—hadn't he said, "If you ever make it to the West Coast, be sure and give me a call"? But I knew I needed more contacts. Most of my time in Durant was spent scratching my head and thinking.

After intense concentration I stretched my imagination to include another "contact" in California. Long ago our high school football team had played a team from Texas. One of its outstanding members, Layne ("Shotgun") Britton, had eventually made his way to California and was working as a makeup man at RKO studios. I had no idea whether he'd even remember my name, but I added *his* name to my contact list.

My mother, being cautious, conservative, and deeply religious, worried about the evils of California. I tried to reassure her by mentioning Shotgun Britton.

"I'll know lots of folks out there, Mom. Why, I'll look up Shot Britton right away. Remember him? He's from this part of the country. I played football against him in high school."

"No," insisted Mom, "I don't remember him at all. Are you sure you do?"

I enlarged on Shotgun's career. "Oh, he was a super player. All-American on the Grantland Rice team. Played at Hardin-Simmons College after high school—first all-American from that school."

"Why's he in California?"

"Makeup man."

"Those film studios might not be a good influence on you, Pinky."

"But Shot Britton might be."

My mother remained doubtful, and truthfully so did I. Apart from my fanciful "reported" agreement with Jimmy Grier, my only other chance was Shot Britton—a long shot, to be sure.

8

Biltmore Bowl

On a crisp fall morning in 1934 I set out to seek my fortune in the company of a fraternity brother and two other friends. The four of us had a total bankroll of $225 plus a Model A Ford. I had a definite goal in going to California—launching my song. The others were simply along for the ride.

The Model A made it across the mountains and deserts of U.S. 66 without any major setbacks. We rolled into Los Angeles at twilight. Looking around, I was amazed at the city of sprawling lights. Bigger and better than I'd expected. I decided to allow myself one night's sleep before hitting the RKO lot to look for Shot Britton.

The next morning I had a pleasant surprise. The day was sunny and clear, and the gates to RKO Studios were wide open. I simply walked onto the lot and asked to see Shot. Then something even more amazing happened: he remembered me. I told him my hopes, and he told me his own findings about California. "Things have a strange way of twisting around out here, Pinky. You never know what you'll end up doing. I came out under contract to MGM to be an actor. Now I'm doing makeup at RKO."

By then I knew he was gaining a reputation as one of the best makeup men in the industry. Some stars wouldn't allow anyone else to apply their makeup. This list eventually included such actors and actresses as Robert Mitchum, Jane Russell, and John Wayne. I was delighted by his success, and I told him my real purpose in coming to see him. "I don't have any thoughts about movies," I said truthfully, "but doesn't RKO have a music publishing company somewhere on the lot?"

"Right over there," he pointed between a sound stage and some orange trees. "The West Coast office of Irving Berlin Music sits right there. The head guy's name is Dave Dreyer. Want me to get you an appointment?"

"Me and my guitar," I answered, astonished at such generosity. I felt that I'd truly arrived in the Garden of Eden and apples were simply falling into my lap.

When Shot Britton finished making the arrangements, I ran—not walked—to see Dave Dreyer. I found a young man with a quick smile and an eager way of nodding his head that radiated energy. He indulged in about two minutes of chitchat and then nodded at my guitar. "OK, kid, demonstrate whatever it is you've got."

It had always been easy for me to perform before an audience, but this one-to-one performance made me nervous. It seemed that the audition was dragging along forever, me singing soulfully into Dave Dreyer's smiling face. Suddenly he interrupted me, "OK, that's enough!"

I was stunned. I had just arrived at the part of the song that goes, ". . . She can go where she wants to go, / do what she wants to do, / I don't care . . . ." My heart froze with anticipation that Dave Dreyer didn't care either. Silently I put my guitar back in its case, figuring his next words would be to ask me to leave.

He looked up, twitched his head, and said matter of factly, "I'll have the contracts drawn up."

"What! You *like* it?"

He was too busy to answer, already pulling apart his desk for forms and signaling his secretary. "Like it?" He barely glanced up. "Oh, sure. It's a winner. Anyone can see that. The contract will be ready today."

I sat down very slowly to avoid falling over. Twenty-four hours in California, and I'd succeeded in getting "Object" published. It took a few minutes for such good news to sink in, and then I saw another possibility. I would certainly look up Jimmy Grier now, having the additional ammunition of a song under contract. I asked Dave Dreyer a favor. "I'm going down to the Biltmore Bowl this afternoon to see an old friend of mine, Jimmy Grier. Would you write him a note telling him your opinion of my song?"

43

Dave managed one of his snap-of-the-head nods, then scribbled on a note pad, handed me the paper, and went on with his work.

I excused myself, floating out of his office as if on a cloud. The note read, "Dear Jimmy, love this song, can't wait to hear you play it." I stuffed the note in my pocket as if it were my life's savings—which is basically what the scrap of paper amounted to.

Armed with the note and my collegiate musical arrangement of "Object," I rode a crosstown bus to the Biltmore Hotel. This imposing hotel was grand by any standards, a deluxe establishment that featured big-name band entertainment in a monstrous room known as the "Bowl." The acoustics in the Bowl were excellent, and it was usually filled to capacity with celebrities and dancers.

When I first walked into the Bowl, however, there was no atmosphere of glamour. It was afternoon, and no one was around but Grier's rehearsal technicians. The tables were uncovered, and the chairs propped up. When Grier walked in, my heart was thudding two hundred beats a minute. I clutched my music, waved my hand, and attempted to look casual. "Hey, Jimmy! What you know, old buddy? Long time, no see!"

I know he was shocked to see me. After all, he'd never seen or heard from me after that incident in Oklahoma several years before. He managed to look only slightly surprised and welcomed me to California. Then I handed him the note from Dave Dreyer and followed with the immediate question, "How about letting me sing with your band?" His mild surprise turned to outright amazement.

First he stood silent, apparently at a loss for words to combat such presumption, and then he shook his head, obviously unimpressed. "You're sort of new out here, boy. I've got acres of singers and batches of songwriters. They're a dime a dozen, and all dying to appear with my band."

I didn't give up. "Then how about having your orchestra try the song? Here—I have complete arrangements."

Again he considered, and then abruptly he held out his hand to take the music, apparently hoping to get rid of me by running through the arrangement quickly. He passed out the sheets to the orchestra members. They looked at each other quizzically, apparently thinking "The Object of My Affection" was a strange title. As they tuned up, they seemed reassured. The melody was normal even if the lyrics were unusual.

The run-through went smoothly, considering that none of the musicians had seen the music before. Grier finished conducting, laid down his baton, and turned to me. He frowned, then smiled, then smacked his lips together in indecision. "Not too bad," he decided, giving a shrug. "Come down tonight, and you can sing it. No promises, understand? Just show up, and we'll see what happens."

"You bet I'll be here. What time?"

"Early."

"Right."

"And Pinky—wear a blue suit."

"A blue suit?" I considered a moment, then decided the old bit about honesty was good as any. "Actually, I own three suits, Jimmy. Two of them happen to be my underwear. I'm standing right here in the middle of my entire wardrobe."

He laughed, reminded me again to be early, and then said, "The band runs through the new numbers at the beginning of the evening before the place fills up."

"That's O.K. with me. I don't mind being a guinea pig for waiters and busboys." I intended to sing "Object" for anyone who would listen. I hurried out of the Biltmore Bowl, aware my number-one order of business was to have my suit pressed at a quick-clean laundry. My second errand was to invest five cents in a telephone call to Shot Britton. I wanted first to thank him for sending me to Dreyer and then to tell him about tonight's chance.

When Shot Britton came on the line, I began yelling enthusiastically, "Shot! Guess what? I got my big chance. Tonight. I'm singing with Grier's band at the Biltmore Bowl!" When he expressed his pleasure that things were turning out well, I asked, "Do you think you can come down and hear me? Maybe round up some of your buddies? I need a friendly audience—some shills who will be sure to clap and whistle when I finish singing."

"I'll give it a try," promised Shot. "But the Biltmore is a pretty far bus ride for most of my friends. We'll come if we can afford it."

"Anyone you can round up! I'll certainly appreciate it."

The rest of the afternoon I checked my watch every ten minutes, remembering I was supposed to be "early." When I did arrive back at the Biltmore, I was early indeed. I beat the entire band. At 7:45 I was in place among sparkling chandeliers, tables with white cloths and fresh flowers, and a crowd of immaculately attired waiters. I went backstage, wondering what kind of audience I'd play to. The early dinner crowd would probably be more interested in food than music. The band usually began playing at eight, and then Grier made his appearance around nine. After that the serious dancing began. In my opinion the acoustics and atmosphere of the Biltmore Bowl could make any singer sound good. But what kind of reception would I get at 8:30 with no audience except the dinner crowd?

Promptly at half past eight the assistant bandleader gave me the signal to come out and do my number. As I marched out, I was dismayed to see that the room was no more than one-fourth full. The guests had been spread throughout the room to accommodate the waiters equally. Playing to such a sparse crowd meant projecting myself in all directions.

I approached the microphone resolutely, hoping that my previous years of bandleading and solo work would give me an air of professionalism. After all, I reasoned, this was *my* song, *my* lyrics, and *my* arrangement. If I couldn't sell it now, no one could.

The orchestra's backup work was as smooth as if we'd rehearsed together for months. I sang heart and soul, mind and body. When I finished, I stepped back and held my breath. The next few seconds would tell me whether to stick around for the second show or turn my face toward Oklahoma. It was a long few seconds, filled with yearning, hope, and fear.

Then the cavernous Biltmore Bowl erupted with applause. The sound was like the roar of a freight train. The audience, although small, went on a rampage of clapping, cheering, and whistling. I watched in disbelief as people stood at their tables, applauding and calling for more. Grateful? Delighted? Those words are the understatements of the century.

Bud Foster, lead singer with the Grier band, congratulated me.

"Do us all a favor," he said graciously. "Sing us another round of 'Object.'"

I did the song three more times before Jimmy Grier arrived at nine. The crowd was still enthusiastic. The band was a hubbub of excitement over the phenomenon. They started telling Grier what had happened. Bud Foster, the singer, went out of his way to praise my song to his boss.

Grier listened, grinned, and commented, "At least your suit is clean." He paused and then said, "If you're doing this well, why don't we plug you into a spot on the second show tonight? You can try out the song on a full house."

"Tonight?" There was only one emotion in my mind—amazement.

"I'll introduce you this time, Pinky. Give you a little buildup and send-off. Any objections?"

"Hardly!" I went backstage to wait out the intermission. I felt that luck and timing were both finally on my side. Sitting in a hardback folding chair, my long legs stuck against the dressing room wall, I closed my eyes. Suddenly I was aware of footsteps. Instantly I was up, facing a tall man with a broad smile.

He introduced himself, "I'm Baron Long." He didn't have to add that he was the owner of the Biltmore Hotel. We shook hands. He said, "Congratulations," sounding as if I'd won a beauty contest.

Grier came into the room. He and Long huddled about plans for the second show. "I have an idea!" exclaimed Long. "Let's call Joe Faber."

While he dialed on the desk phone, I asked Grier, "Who's Joe Faber?"

Grier winked. "Only the next rung up your ladder of overnight success. Faber's the Biltmore publicity chief. The guy who books the entertainers."

"I'd be delighted to meet Mr. Faber," I said solemnly, holding my breath in anticipation.

When Faber arrived, it was apparent to me that he really knew his business. He was full of plans. "We'll get on the phone and get the press over here, gratis, for the second show. I'll call the *Herald Examiner* personally. That means Louella!"

I imagine that everyone in America in 1934 knew about Louella

Parsons. She was the reigning queen of the gossip columnists, a driving force behind much of Hollywood's entertainment publicity. A word, yea or nay, from Louella could mean the beginning or the end of my aspirations. My stomach started churning. It was all I could do to sit still until the second show.

By the time for my appearance in the late show the Bowl was three-fourths full. This time around I rated an introduction. Jimmy Grier stepped up the microphone, told the crowd a bit about me, and concluded, "And here he is—Pinky Tomlin—the Oklahoma Flash!"

Quite an impromptu billing! The Oklahoma Flash! Heck, Jimmy could call me anything he wanted as long as he let me sing.

I launched into my arrangement of "The Object of My Affection" one more time. About the middle of the song my excitement turned to wonder. Was this awesome evening really happening? Two days previously I'd been bouncing across the desert in a Model A with no more prospects for success than those of other dreamers flocking to California. Now, as I finished the second show, I held my emotions tightly, wondering if the ovation of the first show had been merely a fluke. But again the applause burst forth real as thunder. As I took my bows, the cheers and whistles sounded better than bass drums. I hadn't been dreaming after all.

The morning's *Herald Examiner* contained a writeup on the first page of the feature section. In a boxed item Louella Parsons reported in bold print: "Oklahoma Tornado Hits Biltmore Bowl."

So now I was not only a "flash" but a full-fledged twister. Somewhere in all the night's excitement I'd also been given a job at forty dollars a week. With that kind of new security I could afford to be amused by some of the publicity that arose from my opening night's performance. The Biltmore Hotel prided itself on continental sophistication. The Bowl was the largest nightclub in California, the biggest west of Chicago, for that matter. Despite its extravagant image, the hotel publicity department played up the notion that I was some country hick who had wandered in off the streets and started singing.

After Louella Parson's story about me, the other papers picked up the country-boy line. Indeed I had a pretty fair southwestern drawl. Yes, I was new to all Hollywood's glamour and sophistication, but, no, I hadn't stumbled into the Biltmore and opened my mouth and out popped the song. Some of the stories went to silly extremes, billing me as the "hog-calling crooner." One referred to my drawl as "almost indiscernible jargon" full of pronunciations such as "caow" for cow and "hawg" for hog. I was given credit for an abnormal number of y'alls, ain'ts, shuckses, howdies, and reckon-so's in my speech pattern.

None of this bothered me unduly. The fallout from the hayseed publicity was phenomenal, packing the sophisticated Biltmore Bowl night after night. If the dining and dancing public of southern California wanted to think of me as a backwoods bumpkin, it was all right with me. If the country image would draw them to hear me, then I figured they'd make up their own minds when they heard my music.

Despite the nice reviews and the good publicity, I made a few attempts on my own to ensure good audiences. I called the Delta Tau Delta house at UCLA and told the chapter president my schedule. "Do you suppose some of you brothers could come down to the Biltmore and see the show? The Bowl's a big place, but there's no cover charge to get in—no minimum, either."

After my urging the Delts swarmed the place on Friday nights. After the first week I sat down to take stock of what had happened. The main idea in my mind was that America really was rightly billed the "land of opportunity." I had dreams and incentive, yes, but taking a shot at the Biltmore Bowl lay in the realm of land-of-opportunity stories.

I played up this angle to some of the reporters, and they agreed. They also were sharp enough to spot my Delt fraternity ring. One inquired about it, asking, "How do you square all this hog-calling simpleton stuff with a college education and fraternity life?"

I admitted that my background included four years at Oklahoma University and two years of law school, a degree in music, and a fraternity membership. "But I have no reason to object to the ain't-got-no-education-at-all stories, boys. It's like everyone says in show business, 'I don't mind what you say as long as you spell my name *right*—and often.'"

The reporter nodded, being professional enough to see he should leave well enough alone. In some ways I felt exactly as shy and out of place as the stories indicated. Performing at a prom in Oklahoma was considerably different from making it big with the blasé celebrities who swarmed the Biltmore. There were other complex facets to the entertainment business in California that I hadn't even suspected as a member of the Southern Melodians and Boomer Band.

It seemed to my advantage to keep right on saying, "shucks," and singing my heart out. So when Louella Parsons called in person to say she'd liked my show, I replied politely, "Yes, ma'am, I'm much obliged."

Perhaps if I had been more articulate with the press, they might have touched on some of the other qualities that I felt contributed to my success—lucky timing, good health, tremendous desire to make it. I was grateful for all the good things that were happening to me; they confirmed the basic faith I had in myself. But for the reporters there was much more mileage in profiles of a wide-eyed, gangling, grinning country boy.

During these deluges of publicity I found some interesting parts added to my life. Erma Taylor, in a story for *Radio Stars*, managed to change my clean blue suit to a baggy gray one. She credited Jimmy Grier with writing "The Object of My Affection." While she was at it, she said that my life's ambition was to take over my father's law practice! Apparently it didn't bother her that my father, deceased, had been no closer to being an attorney than filling in as deputy marshal in Bryan County. The story reduced the ten-piece Boomer Band to a five-piece ragtag collection of college kids who "played for the simple ranchers and cowmen of Texas." Miss Taylor also invented a wonderful incident in which some music publisher had offered me fifteen hundred dollars for the outright purchase of "Object." To my uneducated credit I supposedly replied, "I reckon that song must be worth more if yore company is willin' t'pay that much money to an unknown writer."

I had a good laugh over that quote, along with some others that were less flattering. My ego is as big as the next guy's—maybe bigger, since I had so much further to come in the creative game. As Noel

A posed photograph of Pinky Tomlin with Virginia Bruce. Note the early 1930's microphone, the blue suit, and fraternity ring.

Coward once remarked, "I love criticism just so long as it's unqualified praise." I had as much need to think positively about myself as most other people, but all this barn-door baloney was in my favor, so I kept silent and grinned a lot.

It was this fluff of the Erma Taylor variety that was feeding me. The Biltmore Bowl was filling up night after night because of the continuing flap of "hayseed hits big town." Perhaps people came simply to gawk at my long legs, pink hair, and country-boy smile. In any event, the "in-person" act was the important thing in show business in 1934. The highest salaries went to the men and women who were able to project to a live audience.

I took those considerations into mind and also considered the possibility of putting together a personal-appearance act. I certainly wanted to see "Object" recorded and played on the radio. My elation over having the Irving Berlin Company publish the sheet music remained. But an in-person act would enlarge my opportunities for success. During my first few weeks at the Biltmore Bowl, I merely toyed with this possibility, however. I was still impressed by the number of celebrities in the audience. One man who was just breaking into show business was Ronald Reagan. He confided to me that he'd brought the current object of his affection, Jane Wyman, to my show. We three became friends in 1934, and that friendship has continued through the years.

Another person connected with the movie industry who happened to see my appearance was Lucien Hubbard. A producer at Metro-Goldwyn-Mayer studios, Hubbard came to catch my act because his daughters had encouraged him. We met briefly after my number and chatted. Hubbard said, "Pinky, I'll get back to you." I had learned enough California show-biz jargon to translate that phrase as meaning, "I'll call you."

The prospect was intriguing, but I didn't have too much hope that Lucien Hubbard would really "get back to me." I had other things on my mind than movie producers, so I didn't spend any time sitting around waiting for him to call.

My free time was devoted to making other contacts and putting together an in-person act.

Fanchon and Marco, a man-and-woman team who had starred on the old vaudeville circuit, came to see me. They had retired from stage performances and now owned and operated the Los Angeles Downtown Paramount Theatre. They asked me a direct question: "Pinky, would you play the Paramount? The starting salary would be $175 a week. We'd double that if you're held over for a second week."

The figures they were lightly talking about sent me into a flurry of excitement. I breathed in sharply. Here it was, a chance to make more money than I'd ever made in a week plus the opportunity to break into the personal-appearance ranks. I asked hopefully, "Would I get my name on the marquee?"

"In lights," Marco assured me.

We shook hands, confirming the deal. There was no written contract, only a verbal agreement that, if by some strange luck I performed for three weeks, there would be the same double salary each time I was held over. I made some quick calculations. Three weeks would mean seven hundred dollars a week! It sounded like the moon *and* the stars might fall into my lap.

9

Country Boy in Los Angeles

Headlining an act is hard work. When you are young and involved in doing what you really want, it's exciting and heady, but it's still hard physical and emotional work. My job at the Paramount called for four performances a day, five on Saturday and Sunday, making a total of thirty appearances a week.

The burden of work in a headline act falls directly on whoever the "in person" may be. There's no straight man, sidekick, back-up chorus, or house orchestra to take the blame if you fall flat. A movie actor follows someone else's directions. A vocalist with a band is cued by the bandleader. But a headliner steps up to the guillotine and offers his own neck to the audience. The blade of disapproval can fall with astonishing rapidity.

But the opposite can happen too. To my delight, my act at the Paramount was successful, making it past the first week and catapulting my salary to $350 a week.

My act followed the basic format of the times. Stage shows were usually built around a formula that included an opening number with a line of chorus girls. The house band would be onstage or in the orchestra pit. Following this big splashy musical number, the next act would usually be a stand-up comic. Third on the program was often a variety act—jugglers, twirlers, skaters, or magicians. Sometimes a dance team took this slot, performing ballroom or ballet-type soft music.

The staff bandleader at most theaters acted as master of ceremonies for the whole show. He would come onstage after the third act and announce, "Now, it's star time! And here comes our headliner!"

54

This fourth position, next to last on the program, was the traditional spot for the big-name performer. After he'd done his act, there was a closer, which again featured the lines of chorus girls, usually with especially gaudy costumes or some gimmick such as trumpets.

My stage act was remarkbly quiet for a headliner. I wore no make-up, dressed in street clothes, and used no props except my guitar. My only trademark was a hat. The audience thought I was simply homespun and ordinary, but the lack of elaborate costumes and props meant that I could save time backstage and didn't need a large dressing room. Besides, a simple wardrobe saved a lot of money.

My basic format was to come on singing, welcome the audience, do some familiar songs, add a little patter, sing a holiday song if appropriate, and then launch my well-known version of "The Object of My Affection." After that, I'd bring out the guitar, put my foot on a milking stool, and do a novelty number. A favorite of the times was "I'll Be Your Sitting Bull and You'll be My Minnie Ha Ha." A few more jokes followed, and then I'd prove I was a musician by doing a serious number such as "I Believe." Finally, I'd thank the audience, and then I'd return in the big finale to take extra bows.

The idea of my act was simplicity itself. But it apparently appealed to a wide range of people, for audiences came to the Paramount not only for the first and second weeks but for the third, fourth, and fifth. Obviously doubling my salary each week was out of the question, but Fanchon and Marco generously agreed to $1,000 a week after the fifth week. Then, when I'd run for ten weeks, they went to $1,250. This was to be "for the duration," which no one could guess. A run of two or three weeks was considered good in 1934. Ten weeks was phenomenal, and there seemed no end in sight as lines outside the Paramount stretched for a block and a half before every performance. No one knew how long I'd keep drawing a crowd.

A stage show was a bargain in 1934. The cost of a ticket was forty cents. For that price an audience at the Paramount saw the high-kicking routines of the Fanchonettes, a comic, the dance act of Bill ("Bojangles") Robinson, and me.

As the holiday season of 1934 approached, I added Christmas songs to my act, wondering if I'd be held over after the new year. If I'd had a

Theater marquee for a stage show. This appearance was in Chicago, but the billing was similar to that used by the Downtown Los Angeles Paramount. The price of admission was forty cents after six P.M.

crystal ball, I would have seen that my run at the Paramount would stretch nearly to Easter—twenty weeks in all.

Around Christmastime I received an urgent call from Louella Parsons. "Pinky, you have to come down and do the Mount Sinai benefit."

I didn't know what Mount Sinai was, but I knew not to turn down Miss Parsons. Her command meant a prompt, "Yes, ma'am," with no questions asked.

"Shrine Auditorium," she instructed me, giving the date and time. "Will you be there?"

"In my best bib and tucker," I agreed.

"I've lined up a fine group for the Mount Sinai benefit this year. You'll be in good company with Shirley Temple, Joe E. Brown, Dick Powell, Will Rogers, and Irvin S. Cobb."

On the night of the benefit I discovered that I was to be introduced by Mr. Cobb. He was one of the alternate masters of ceremonies. In those days Irvin S. Cobb was an accepted figure as a philosopher, humorist, short-story writer, and actor. His acting was of questionable quality, though Twentieth Century Studios had used him in several pictures with Will Rogers. There was no question about his humor, however. He once said of producers, "They're like goldfish. They can swim around with their eyes open and still be asleep." Another time he hit on a truth of the writing and entertainment worlds: "A good storyteller is a person who has a good memory and hopes other people haven't."

Mr. Cobb and I met backstage and discussed my introduction and the material I would do. For some reason—perhaps to boost his reputation as a humorist—he then "forgot" all our plans. He completely ignored the introduction we'd rehearsed. Instead, he gestured to the orchestra leader to provide a big fanfare for me, and then said loudly, "And now, folks, our next guest is Pinky—uh—er—STINKY Tomlin!"

I was already walking on stage. A chorus of satirical laughter welled up from the huge Shrine Auditorium audience. I'm sure I looked taken aback at his sudden switch of lines. Apparently he decided he could get some more laughs out of my country-boy walk. He grabbed the microphone and pointed at me, raising his voice to a yodel, "Well, hi there, farmer!"

I made up my mind to give as much as I had to take from him. I responded, "Well, hi, neighbor," implying he was in the same farmer category. Both lines drew laughter. My answer received a slightly better response.

Cobb then derided me by saying, "Uh-oh, folks, we got us a smart aleck here!"

I played straight man to that. "No, sir, I sure don't aim to be."

"Maybe you don't know what we do with smart alecks out here in California, farmer."

"I sure don't, but I know what we do with cobs back in Oklahoma."

The Shrine Auditorium shook to the ceiling with laughter. This audience wasn't so far removed from country humor not to know the old joke about poor folks unable to afford a Sears catalog for outhouse paper. The play on Irvin Cobb's name delighted them. The bedlam of applause and laughter lasted several minutes.

After the corncob joke Mr. Cobb didn't fool around with me anymore. He left the stage, and I tried to do my song, but neither the audience nor I could quit laughing. I made it halfway through "The Object of My Affection" and then broke up. "Aw, heck," I apologized, "you all know the rest of the song anyhow!"

I made my exit to another round of friendly laughter. Backstage I saw Will Rogers sitting in the wings, awaiting his turn. He was doing a country-boy act too, sitting hunkered down in a crouch. He winked at me. "We told him, didn't we, boy?"

The papers carried sanitized versions of the Cobb story the next morning. In 1934 the margins of acceptable journalism, even Hollywood sex and scandal gossip, were considerably narrower than today. For many years afterward, I had to explain what really happened at the Mount Sinai benefit.

I came off the winner in the press releases according to Louella Parsons and her cohorts. It is hard to believe how important such trivia was in show business in 1934, but a mention in the *Examiner* was worth thousands of dollars. Among entertainers the worst thing was not false or misleading information about you but the silent treatment. Louella's little boxes of gossip regularly rated the front page of the feature section in Mr. Hearst's paper. In 1938, when Hedda Hopper became Louella's great rival, the age of show-business gossip reached its zenith. With Louella at the *Examiner* and Hedda at the *Los Angeles Times*, the nation was treated to twice-daily doses of trivia. This battle of the gossip queens was helped along by the ladies themselves, the studios, and the stars.

In 1934, though, Louella reigned alone. She was backstage at the Mount Sinai benefit, congratulating herself and her stars. When the benefit was over, all the performers were treated to champagne and sandwiches. An entertainer actually sings for his supper at a charity show.

During the after-show party Will Rogers came over to me again. He was still chuckling over the cob joke. We talked awhile, easily and naturally, coming from the same background. We both used country-boy images and styles. I told him that his famous statement about never meeting a man he didn't like bothered me. "Is that really true, Will? Because I've sure met a bunch I didn't like at all."

He drawled, "Well, young man, you and me are from the same part of the country. We both know everyone that pulls on britches ain't no man."

Will then proceeded to give me some advice as an established entertainer to a newcomer. "Pinky, I've heard your singin', and I've tried to make out what you was sayin' when you talked."

"And what's your verdict?" I asked, figuring he was going to tell me to drop the talking.

"Talkin' is the best part of your act."

I was astounded, thinking my real talent lay with music.

"Yep," he insisted, "based on my way of thinkin', if you talk long enough, you're bound to say somethin'."

10

Bill ("Bojangles") Robinson

One other interesting story grew out of the Mount Sinai benefit. My friend, Bill ("Bojangles") Robinson was in the audience that night. Normally he would have been onstage as a performer, but he'd recently undergone an appendectomy and was still recovering. He and I had worked together at the downtown Paramount Theatre, and he was one of my first friends in show business.

When I threw the cob joke at Irvin Cobb, Bill Robinson was probably the man who laughed the hardest. He later insisted that he had done the classic trick of laughing so hard he'd popped a stitch in his appendectomy scar. To say the least, he liked the joke.

I remembered his affection for this gag later when he built a beautiful new home in Los Angeles. When he held a formal open house, it seemed that a housewarming gift was in order. Bill and I had shared some wonderful moments, both onstage and off, so I wanted something especially meaningful.

After careful consideration, I constructed a unique present for his new home. The gift was a solid mahogany box with a clear-glass front. Mounted inside the frame was a V-shape support. On the bracket I placed two corncobs, one red and one white. Outside I anchored a small hammer and the sign "In case of emergency, break glass." Naturally the gift was a big hit. Bill placed it in the guest bath of the pool cabana.

Looking back, I find it interesting to see the changes in relationships between blacks and whites in the last fifty years. In many ways the entertainment industry was significantly ahead of its times in race relations. Before he died in 1949, Bill Robinson had become both a millionaire and a beloved performer, but he still had to build his elegant home in the "colored" section of Los Angeles. He was able to kid about it, but the jokes were aimed at the bigotry that still surrounded his people.

His nickname, "Mr. Bojangles," is of uncertain origin, despite many press-release stories about its derivation. Bill's background was well known. He was born a grandson of slaves in 1878 in the poorest section of Richmond, Virginia. He was reared by his grandmother and joined a road show when he was nine-years old. After dancing in the nightclubs of the South, he went on to Broadway and then the movies. One of his most famous performances was with Shirley Temple in *The Little Colonel*, where he did the classic dance on the staircase.

Another of Robinson's hits was *Stormy Weather*, in which he starred with Lena Horne and Cab Calloway. It was my pleasure to write a song for that picture. "My, My, Ain't That Somethin'" was the come-on song that Cab sang to Lena and was used again in the big finale number.

When Bill and I were playing the downtown Paramount, we developed a duo routine that audiences loved. After we'd finished our respective solo acts, we'd come out together for a short encore. Bill would sing, "The object of my affection can change my complexion / from brown to rosy red . . ." while I would do my version of his famous time-step dance routine. We'd exit together, performing a wild truckin'-on-down dance that was quite a crowd pleaser.

We were such a success as a team that we played several bookings together. One engagement was set for Boston, Massachusetts. That was three thousand miles from Bill's home base in California and meant a flight on an airliner. Cross-country flights were still something of a novelty in the 1930s. Bill was opposed to the whole concept of air travel, but the schedule was such that we had to fly or cancel. Bill was nervous at the airport. "Pinky," he admitted, "I'm flat-out scared!"

I tried to reassure him. "It's not all that high. Why, about twelve thousand feet is tops for aircraft."

"I don't care how high we go if I can keep one foot on the ground."

I wanted to play the date in Boston. I spent a long time trying to dispel his fears. "There's no reason to be afraid, Bill. After all, if it's not your time to go, everything will be OK."

"I know that. But what if we're dangling up there at twelve thousand feet, and it's the *pilot's* time to go?"

Bill and I finally got on the plane. Wouldn't you know it—engine trouble. We had to land in Denver for repairs. He was doubly nervous when we finally took off again—same story, second verse—more trouble. We landed in Chicago. Bill was in a state of panic. I doubted that we'd get to Boston. Eventually we made it, but the experience marked Bill. Later he used the material as part of his comedy act, but he certainly wasn't laughing at the time. One of the reasons he and I discontinued our combined act was that he never did reconcile himself to the friendly skies.

Many years after his death in 1949, Richmond, Virginia, erected a statue to Mr. Bojangles. In 1973 the city dedicated a 9½-foot aluminum representation of Robinson in mid dance step, recreating his dance on the staircase. The statue is at the corner of Chamberlayne Parkway and Leigh and Adams streets, not too far from where Bill was born. It's nice to think he'll always dance on the streets of his hometown. It's even nicer to know that he was able to laugh at the prejudice that surrounded the black entertainers of his day.

One of his famous stories indicates the humor he was able to find in bigotry. It concerned the time he was playing the top theater in Atlanta, Georgia. The policy of this elegant theater was that no blacks were allowed in the lower-level seats. "Balcony Only" was the traditional rule for blacks in the audience.

During one of Robinson's appearances a small black child was hanging over the balcony railing. The child slipped, falling all the way to the lower-level seats. The child's mother stood up and yelled loudly, "Git yourself out of them expensive seats and back up here where you belong!"

Bill Robinson was a fine human being and one of my earliest and closest friends among entertainers. May he dance in peace on the streets of Richmond and on the golden staircase of Heaven.

11

Records and Radio

The business of making phonograph records was in its infancy in 1934. The bulky wax recordings were not as popular as sheet music. A record played over the radio might generate a little demand for the record, but the big impact was on sheet-music sales. A hit recording sometimes sold as many as fifty thousand copies, but sheet music sales sometimes soared above half a million.

The record industry is now a multibillion-dollar-a-year monster full of electronic gadgetry and sophisticated promotions. In 1934 only about ten companies were making records. As for the money involved, it's necessary only to say that the standard advance was fifty dollars a side or union scale. The big-name recording companies were Brunswick and Victor. Subsidiary labels included Edison, Velvatone, and Conqueror. Jack Capp, president of Brunswick and later of Decca, had signed such talent as Bing Crosby, the Andrews Sisters, Tony Martin, Russ Colombo, and the Boswell Sisters to record for his company. Over at Victor, Leonard Joy put Johnny Marvin under contract. This idea of "exclusive" contracts was fairly new. Before the mid-thirties a performer could cut records for any company that asked him—even record the same song on different labels.

Behind the scenes, RCA had a monopoly on all the electronic equipment, such as microphones and recorders. This dominance wasn't broken until the antitrust suits of the 1950s.

In later decades even the names of musical types changed. What we call today country-and-western music was known then as hillbilly or cowboy. Ragtime came close to being country music too, including piano, drums, banjo, and a hoedown fiddle. Hillbilly, or ragtime cowboy, played loudly in honkytonks, country roadhouses, and other places lonely cowboys passed the long evenings. A real tearjerker for a guy who was slightly broke and slightly drunk was "Ace in the Hole."

Soul music made its mark in the thirties but went under the undisguised label "race records." Sweet or pop music was anything that relied on a twelve- to eighteen-piece orchestra with emphasis on the violins. This kind of music went over big at country clubs, hotel ballrooms, and college parties. The big names were Freddie Martin and Guy Lombardo.

Among the "big" bands, or swing bands, the biggest and best were Benny Goodman's, Glenn Miller's, Harry James's, and the Dorseys'. Artie Shaw, Les Brown, Duke Ellington, Count Basie, and Glen Gray's Casa Loma Orchestra were superstar bands that rated center stage. My favorite during this period was Jimmy Lunsford. For some reason, his organization lasted only about four years.

The big bands used their bandleader's specialties as their signatures. Harry James and his trumpet, Benny Goodman and his clarinet, and drummers Buddy Rich and Gene Krupa all hit the star ranks. The swing bands usually had headline girl vocalists too, such as Anita O'Day, Martha Tilton, Betty Hutton, and Doris Day.

Through the years I cut about fifty different two-sided records, mostly on the Brunswick label. I recorded an album for Decca entitled "Ragtime Cowboy Joe." Almost all my records were my own songs. Of course, my first record was "The Object of My Affection." The recording session was at a private studio used exclusively by Brunswick. Jimmy Grier was staff conductor, and his orchestra did the accompaniment.

The setup was fairly advanced for 1934. We had a soundproof studio, sound technicians, and microphones. There were none of today's refinements, such as mixers, tracks, or tapes. If the singer or orchestra made a mistake, everything came to a halt, and you began all over again. Sometimes it would take eight or ten tries to get a take. I was lucky in that I had a good ear for music and excellent intonation, and this let me key in quickly at recording sessions. Nelson Riddle once complimented me by saying, "Pinky, you're one of the few singers I know who can be counted on to do a one-take on any record."

My voice sounded strange to me when I heard it played back on a record. Normally I had a pretty good range from second tenor to medium baritone, almost two octaves, but the early-day records made all male voices sound high-pitched. Even Bing Crosby sometimes came off sounding like a boy soprano.

It was a feather in my musical cap that I'd been allowed to record "Object." Normally a songwriter stepped aside and let someone else sing his creations on radio and records. I've often thought "Object" was a success partly because it was noticed under superlative conditions at the Biltmore Bowl and partly because I was lucky enough to record it personally. Over the years there have been various recordings made of the song, but I have remained closely associated with both words and music. Bing Crosby once insisted, "No one can sing 'Object' like Pinky!" Some people have even told me they think my association with the song is almost a legend.

I'm the first to admit that an easily identified song serves a songwriter and entertainer very well. Bing Crosby, Kate Smith, Bob Hope, and Al Jolson all took advantage of the theme-song format. None of them had the privilege of composing and introducing their own material as their signature songs. I think my greatest career asset was this ability to produce original material.

Another first in entertainment records that has been credited to me is the rule, No service during the show. This means the customer is expected to arrive in the lounge, ballroom, or supper club, have drinks and dinner, and then settle back and listen to the performer. This format is advantageous to the audience, service staff, and entertainer. The setup hasn't always been so clear. For years the person in the spotlight had to compete with waiters banging trays and cocktail waitresses prancing the aisles. No service during the show became immensely popular with all segments of the entertainment industry. It is now added to nearly every performer's contract.

Many of my friends in show business have told me how important this rule has been to their careers. Nat King Cole found that his soft, intimate styling went over much better when he didn't have to battle ongoing distractions. It was Cole who took the no-service-during-the-show clause to Las Vegas, when he appeared at a main hotel room there. If you've visited Las Vegas lately, you know the rule is still in effect. Everything comes to a halt for the show. In my opinion that's exactly the way it should be.

After my record of "Object" was released, I wrote two more songs that I performed for Brunswick. Both featured catchy, unusual titles: "What's the Reason I'm Not Pleasin' You?" and "The Love Bug Will Bite You If You Don't Watch Out." Those songs were written in the same popular vein as other novelty hits of the thirties, such as "I Found a Million Dollar Baby in a Five and Ten Cent Store" and "Let's Have Another Cup of Coffee, Let's Have Another Cup of Tea."

Many people have asked me how I go about the process of writing a song. Rarely if ever have I waited for the much-talked-about thing called inspiration. I was always moved by much more businesslike forces, such as conditions of the market, reflections of the era, and the need for holiday themes.

Find a catchy title and build a musical story around it—that's the easiest way for me to write a song. "The Object of My Affectcion" came out of a lawbook. I conceived "The Love Bug Will Bite You if You Don't Watch Out" from hearing the old folk saying, "The goblins will getcha if you don't watch out." I combined this with the popular expression, "The golf bug's got me." I felt that a warning about the love bug would be logical.

Almost all songs had long, involved, logical verses to accompany the snappy chorus. The verse explained and set up the refrain. For "Love Bug" I wrote:

Listen all you people, you'd better be aware
Love's an epidemic and it's in the air
It's a thing that gets you even tho you're very smart
So take my advice, go out and vaccinate your heart,

'Cause the love bug will bite you if you don't watch out,
and if he ever bites you, you will sing and shout.
You'll go la la da da de da da and wo de do de do . . .

© 1937, Joy Music, Inc.

In some of my songs the lyrics practically wrote themselves once I had the basic rhyme scheme in mind. Considerable editing and rearranging was necessary for others. Most professional songwriters rely on editing rather than inspiration for salable songs. As in many other creative fields, it's perspiration over inspiration 90 percent of the time.

Another part of the record business in the early days was the practice of having the performer plug his song. This practice has changed little over the years, differing now only in degree and sophistication. In the thirties most music publishing companies had song pluggers who worked under the title "publisher's representative." Their job was to visit radio stations, music stores, and bandleaders. A song plugger would get a list of the songs his company intended to make hits, and then he'd go to hotels and clubs and see the bandleader, the vocalist, or some other name headliner who was playing the entertainment room. Besides asking the vocalist to be sure to sing the number, the song plugger would offer to make up special arrangements of the music for the orchestra. Most of the large bands were heard on radio, either locally or nationally, and the result was good exposure of a song on the airwaves.

Radio was the medium of the thirties, though subsidiary sales were focused on sheet music. Song pluggers were exactly right when they said that radio "had the nation by the ears." The chain of demand was indirect. The public heard the song on the radio and then went to the music stores and purchased sheet music. Disc jockeys had a lot of power, then as now, when they decided which records to play and plug.

Another option for songwriters was to cut in a star singer or bandleader on the royalties in return for help in recording a song. Over the years I have done several collaborations with such friends as Harry Tobias and Johnny Mercer. In my early days, though, I listed some songs as "collaborations" when really I had given away part of the income to get the song pushed. I figured half a loaf was better than none.

Another way to keep your name alive was to visit the radio stations yourself. Performers did guest appearances wherever the song plug-gers could arrange them. This isn't much different from the contem-porary scene, except that today television, instead of radio, is the place to go.

People tend to forget exactly how powerful radio was during the Depression and World War II eras. *Everyone* kept up with the name of Helen Trent's newest love on the soap opera. *Everyone* knew what time to tune in Gabriel Heatter and the news. *Everyone* waited breathlessly for those fabulous sound effects to emanate from Fibber McGee's over-stuffed closet.

Performers on radio became closely associated and identified with their sponsors. Eddie Cantor starred in "Texaco Star Theatre," Bing Crosby had "Kraft Music Hall," and Lucky Strike cigarettes spon-sored "Your Hit Parade."

Jimmy Grier's band was on national radio three times a week, so while I continued performing at the Biltmore Bowl I was getting good coast-to-coast radio exposure. Locally the Los Angeles station KFI carried the Biltmore show. Together I managed air appearances six times a week. Jimmy Grier also had a commercial radio show for MJB Coffee. This show featured Mary Boland and Charlie Ruggles. Grier spotlighted me several times.

Radio was a springboard for many personalities to launch them-selves in the movies. Airwave popularity regularly was translated into a movie contract. Fibber McGee and Molly moved from their famous half-hour comedy routine into a movie entitled *This Way, Please.* Oth-ers who moved between radio and movies included Phil Harris and Alice Faye, Burns and Allen, Jack Benny, and Bing Crosby. Musical groups from local stations were picked up for featured roles in Hol-lywood productions. George Gobel was a ukelele player on "National Barn Dance" from 1931 to 1934. Al Clauser and his Oklahoma Out-laws on station WHO, Des Moines, were featured in the film *Rootin', Tootin' Rhythm.*

My biggest thrill in radio was when I was asked to appear on Bing Crosby's "Kraft Music Hall." I sang "Object"—a three-minute stint—and earned a thousand dollars. Bing was great to me, giving me a nice personal pitch and later doing my song himself. We were friends for many years; he introduced or sang at least a dozen of my songs during this time.

Most radio music shows featured resident players or hired guest comics. This provided a change of pace between songs. Bing Crosby's usual comic was Bob Burns, who was billed as the "Arkansas Hillbilly." Burns's job was to make down-home jokes about Van Buren, Arkansas, and play the bazooka. His musical contraption was made of lead pipe, sounded funny, and complemented his corny humor. At the end of his bazooka solos he would drop the instrument on the floor, making a horribly loud noise. That always brought a laugh and furnished him with exit applause. Later Burns transferred to the movies for the 1937 film *Mountain Music*.

Another popular show, Eddie Cantor's "Texaco Star Theatre," was basically vaudeville transferred to radio. The format was the old-time minstrel show. About the only straight comedy show that didn't feature musical interludes was Fibber and Molly. Even Jack Benny exploited his talent for violin playing, capitalizing on the idea that he couldn't play at all. Dennis Day provided the vocal talent on the Benny show. Dennis Day later recorded a jingle for Westinghouse entitled "The Laundromat Song." It was written by Harry Tobias, Charley Kisco, and me. As a sample of its unforgettable lyrics,

You don't need a beautiful setting
For love to get a start
Just let me tell you my love story
Where and when I lost my heart.

I met her at the corner laundromat
We had a little chat down at the laundromat
And in between our clothes were gettin' clean,
To the swish, swish, swish of the laundromat machine.
You'd never think romance would blossom here
It never would appear romance could blossom here
But here's the theme that put us on the beam
'Twas the swish, swish, swish of the laundromat machine.

69

THE OBJECT OF MY AFFECTION

We ironed out all our future plans
How those wedding bells did ring
Then the years brought souvenirs of love and everything
Ole Man Stork keeps knockin' at our door
He never seems to tire of knockin' at our door
By gosh! Our wash is growin' more and more
What with Hazel, Jimmy, Mary, Tommy, Susie,
*   Joseph, Joan, and Pat—*
We had to buy the laundromat!

12

Times Square Lady

You can't work in the entertainment industry of southern California without casting at least a wishful eye toward Hollywood. In the 1930s moviemaking was in its infancy despite its loud claims of "Gable is King" and "Long live Tinseltown." Movies, radio, songwriting, and personal appearances overlapped.

Nevertheless, I was still surprised when movie producer Lucien Hubbard made good on his promise to "get back to me." His comment at the Biltmore Bowl had been casual, and so when he called and said, "Pinky, this is Lucien, getting back to you on this MGM business," I really had no specific idea what he wanted.

Of course, I was interested. Lucien Hubbard had come up through the ranks of the movie business. He'd done an adaptation of the Zane Grey novel *The Vanishing American* for Paramount. He was on schedule to produce *Operator 13*, starring Gary Cooper, for MGM. He was just on the verge of big time. I listened intently to his proposal.

"Can you drop by the studio this week, Pinky?" he asked. "Do a screen test? We've got a cute little script we're using as a vehicle for Robert Taylor and Virginia Bruce. It's called *Times Square Lady*. Maybe we could write in a part for you if things work out. You'd sing, play your banjo, whatever."

The movies—all the time I was saying yes to Hubbard, I was thinking how my luck and timing were staying with me. Hollywood was growing by leaps and reels, cranking out hundreds of movies a year. It had been only six years since the talkies had arrived. The film industry was hard at work trying to bring excitement and glamour to a nation that was deep in an economic depression. The daily news-

71

papers were hip-deep in stories of alphabet-soup relief agencies, FDR's "brain trust," and continuing drought in the Midwest. The movies offered a fifteen-cent option on fantasy. For two hours the real world could be held in abeyance while the viewer lost himself in such fluff as *Don't Bet on Blondes* with Errol Flynn.

Hollywood's heyday of romance was the early thirties. I think this was because the nation was so hungry for anything sweet. A vicarious taste of sugar, lavishness, excitement, and love was lapped up by starving audiences. When Mickey Rooney and Judy Garland gazed at each other over milkshakes at the corner drugstore, all America knew they were meant for each other. Times were hard, and that made the screen fairy tales all the more satisfying. Shirley Temple with her baby-sweet dimples and sugarplum smile was easily the hottest new star in years. On the other hand, a touch of sin and well-shielded sex appealed to audiences. Barbara Stanwyck's *Woman in Red* for Warner's Studios hit the right combination of wickedness and crime all done up in a glossy package. As for fantasy, 1933 was the year Gary Cooper was cast as the White Knight in *Alice in Wonderland*.

The year I went to Hollywood for a screen test was a busy one for the movie industry. Of course, there were plenty of tourist traditions already associated with Hollywood—the footprints in cement at Grauman's Chinese Theatre, the big "HOLLYWOOD" sign perched on the hillside above the village, and the dime maps that directed you to homes of such stars as Carole Lombard and Robert Montgomery. Personally I hadn't found the time or the extra money to be a tourist. For the first few months I was in California I wore only my plain blue suit and took only seven-cent streetcar rides to and from work at the Paramount and Biltmore.

It was basically new territory for me to enter the Metro-Goldwyn-Mayer lot and ask for Lucien Hubbard. The studio's geographic location was out in the country, a half day's trip down dirt roads and over hillsides full of orange orchards. The famous Hollywood Hills weren't famous yet, containing only a few white bungalows perched on precarious stilts. I'd heard plenty of stories about the entertainment industry's penchant for "hot and cold running blondes," but I also knew that most folks trying to break into show business lived frugally and rode streetcars. Two other young bachelors I knew shared an apartment while pounding on the doors of Hollywood—Cary Grant and Randolph Scott.

When I arrived at MGM, I was completely ignorant of the intricacies of a sound stage. The motion pictures were filmed in monstrous-sized barns plastered with stucco on the outside and plastered with microphones and hot lights inside.

A studio was a self-contained world. It had its own jargon too, so I received a quick lesson in learning a foreign language. I was unfamiliar with such basic film directions as take, cut, and print, but what did impress me was the energy level and excitement surrounding all the activity. Technicians were scurrying, setting up lights, cameras, and mikes. Make up men dabbed pancake on actors. Crews took down walls, set up furniture, and moved whole rooms within the big barn.

My session at MGM followed a full afternoon's work at the Paramount. I was tired, as usual, after performing. I felt almost numb, following directions with as much spunk as a robot. Fortunately the instructions weren't hard to understand: "Stand on those white lines, Pinky. Look at the lights. Hold your guitar a little lower. Jut your chin at a forty-five-degree angle."

Luckily Hubbard didn't want me to do anything special. "Sing your song, and you can go home," he told me. "You've got a nice natural approach anyway. We'll just leave it alone."

Relieved, I began breathing easier. Singing "Object" came as naturally to me as grinning. I was used to performing the song five to ten times a day. Surely this couldn't be too hard. The only people around to watch were Hubbard and my old friend and accompanist Claude Kennedy. All right, I thought, there's nothing to be scared of here. This is just one more run-through of material that I'm completely familiar with.

I sang the song, turning at various angles as Hubbard told me to. That was it. No fanfare, trumpets, crowds, or chorus girls. Hubbard briskly called thanks in my direction then ordered all the lights turned off. "Pinky, I'll get back to you."

My screen test at Metro-Goldwyn-Mayer was a low-key affair. I sang only one song. Claude Kennedy accompanied me.

I'd heard that line before, but to my surprise, a week later the call from Hubbard came. This time he asked me to come to the studio and talk about a contract.

Again I made the trip to the boondocks and negotiated my own deal. That was long before the day of high-powered agents, multi-million-dollar deals, and percentages of the gross. The standard film took thirteen weeks to produce with standard actor's pay of $150 a week. I felt lucky to be able to get $1,000 a week for the full thirteen-week contract.

Once I was under contract, I thought I'd have a lot to learn. But Hubbard insisted again, "Leave well enough alone. We'll simply plug you into a spot on *Times Square Lady* and let nature take its course."

Acting consisted mainly of learning to control my eyes and head. I wore glasses and a hat, and so most of the time I was "covered" on both counts.

Times Square Lady was typical of the romantic fare of the thirties. The story capitalized on the team of Robert Taylor and Virginia Bruce, who had been a hit together in *Society Doctor*. Their job was to provide the glamour and romance. My job was to be myself. The credits for the picture billed me as "Pinky Tomlin, Durant, Oklahoma."

The story line combined a gambling syndicate, a nightclub, a New York City locale, and plenty of shots of gorgeous Virginia Bruce. The plot was simple. She inherited some night spots, including a skating rink and sports arena, and then tried to clean them up, running them herself and getting rid of the syndicate thugs.

I wasn't sure how my country-boy humor and music were supposed to fit into this big-city epic. I had enough sense to stay quiet about the subject. It was screenwriters Albert Cohen and Robert Shannon who had to come up with a way to work me into the film.

Times Square Lady was filmed in six weeks during December, 1934, and January 1935. The music was prerecorded, and then the sound was played back as we filmed. I had to learn the fine old art of lip-sync, which means fitting the motions of the lips to the music. In *Times Square Lady* I sang "The Object of My Affection" to leading lady Virginia Bruce and "What's the Reason I'm Not Pleasin' You?" to a

Robert Taylor and Virginia Bruce played the romantic leads in *Times Square Lady*. My billing was "Pinky Tomlin, Durant, Oklahoma."

In most movies I sang to the leading lady. In *Times Square Lady*, I crooned "What's the Reason I'm Not Pleasin' You?" to a cow. In Chicago the local press doubted I knew how to milk a cow. I arranged to have a cow delivered to the front of the Oriental Theatre and then performed the chore I'd mastered as a farm boy.

cow. The lip-sync process gives you a standard "one, two, three, four, *bump*" count to get ready. Then you open your mouth, though no sound comes out. You are essentially engaged in silent moviemaking, taping before the cameras but without sound.

The purpose of the movie, like almost all other entertainment efforts that year, was to cash in on all the current themes. It played around with the flaming-youth cult, big-time gambling, the Horatio Alger success formula, the liberated-woman syndrome, and country-boy-sees-the-bright-lights. The film used every word in vogue at the time, with the lines of dialogue full of crooners, swains, vamps, skedaddle, mosey, and hightail it outa here, boy.

Producer Hubbard and director George B. Seitz gave me little advice. They felt that I was already established as a "natural" type. I was told to keep the quiet, shy, hayseed image and not to tamper with my supposedly homey and bashful appeal. My act consisted of playing and singing my own material, so they used this facet as well. Similarly, my name was already pretty well known. For me there was never a question of a movie name.

Most performers ditched their real names in favor of improvements. Leonard Slye became Dick Weston, then later Roy Rogers. Marion Morrison decided to be "Singin' Sandy," the cowboy, but when it became apparent that Sandy couldn't sing, Morrison opted for the name John Wayne. John Crawford started out as dancer Lucille Le Sueur, Doris Day was really Doris Von Kapelhof, Duke Ellington was born Edward Kennedy, and Sheila Ryan started life as Catherine Elizabeth McLaughlin. Another young dancer on the lot began her career as Margarita Carmen Cansino—you probably remember her better as Rita Hayworth.

But Pinky Tomlin was a name deemed worthy of leaving alone. It was easy to remember, fit well on a marquee, and stood out in print because of the Y on the end. William Hazlitt remarked, "A nickname is the hardest stone the devil can throw at a man." I disagree. Nature's trick of giving me a pink complexion and hair presented me with a built-in nickname that gave me built-in recognition as a performer.

The fact that my name was already recognizable was why they billed me as myself in the movie. There's a code to where your name appears in the credits, how big it is, and how often it rolls around. There are little signals associated with the words "starring," "featuring," "introducing," and "with" on the billboard. As all entertainers learn early, "It's not just the name, it's the size of the lights on the marquee."

I was treated well in *Times Square Lady*. The publicity crew locked onto the idea that I was simply having a wonderful time "doing what comes naturally." They had a heyday with the hayseed stories. Their press releases read "Oklahoma Farmer Boy Sensational New Film Personality of the Year" and "You Can't Be Blue When You Hear Pinky Tomlin, New Screen Find, Sing His Own Song Hits."

After all the blarney and the baloney were discounted, the film emerged as a reasonably decent piece of entertainment. The basic story was of an Iowa girl, Toni Bradley, who leads a sheltered life as the daughter of one of New York's nightlife bosses. Then, when her father dies suddenly, she inherits the enterprises. She goes to New York, is resented by her father's henchmen, is pursued by gangsters, is threatened by bodyguards, and is protected by Steve Gordon. The bad guys are outwitted, the heroine falls into the hero's arms, and a happy ending lights up the screen. In the hype of the day, *Times Square Lady* was billed as a "thrilling, fast-moving comedy drama."

The stars, Virginia Bruce and Robert Taylor, were experienced film makers. They and Isabel Jewell showed me tricks of the trade that eased my way into movie work. The writers worked out the storyline so that I portrayed an Oklahoma boy, a country truck driver. In the movie I go to Los Angeles, sing a couple of my songs in a swanky nightclub, am a dismal failure, and then later return to become a great success. Sound familiar? I didn't have to refresh my memory to play those scenes.

The publicity crew got some mileage out of my song, too, using the tag line "First her millions, then her heart made her the object of his affections." Another quick summary read, "Romance, music, and murder thrills as a beauty from Iowa teaches the triple cross to double crossing Broadway." My part in all this was to be funny and romantic at the same time. An anonymous title maker at MGM dubbed me the "hog-callin' crooner."

Isabel Jewell was a fine character actress. She played my girlfriend in my first movie. During filming, she helped me learn the business, teaching me such technicalities as long shots, closeups, and camera angles.

Virginia Bruce was the classic beauty of the thirties—tall and blonde with a sweet face and plenty of figure for those inevitable black, low-cut dresses. She was originally from Fargo, North Dakota, but had been in Hollywood several years, long enough to start a career, retire to marry John Gilbert, divorce him after two years, and recoup her acting stardom with such hits as *Jane Eyre*, *Shadow of Doubt*, and *Society Doctor*.

Society Doctor was the first pairing of Virginia Bruce and newcomer Robert Taylor. In this film they played a nurse and an intern who fell in love. The country, in return, fell in love with them. MGM saw *Times Square Lady* as a sequel of sorts, playing up the idea of "The lovers of *Society Doctor* together again!"

Robert Taylor was a little over a year out of Pomona College. Originally from Filley, Nebraska, with the real name Spangler Arlington Brough, Taylor had already made a name for himself as a dashing, romantic hero bound for stardom. I found him a hardworking, enjoyable guy; we began a friendship on *Times Square Lady* that lasted many years.

Bob Taylor was under contract as a studio player at a salary of $150 a week. Before *Society Doctor* he had done a series of shorts proving that "crime doesn't pay." For *Times Square Lady* the publicity department went all out to cash in on his dark good looks. The posters read, "It took a small town girl to teach him how to love," and "He was too smart to fall in love until he met the Times Square Lady!"

Theaters arranged contests in which the audience could win free tickets to the movie by compiling a list of famous squares, such as Times Square, Herald Square, Washington Square, and Union Square. Metro-Goldwyn-Mayer also produced a sixteen-inch record for radio play that featured my songs "The Object of My Affection" and "What's the Reason I'm Not Pleasin' You?" The records were sent free to radio stations. The general public could buy the record for three dollars.

Irving Berlin Company published the sheet music for both songs, using covers that played up the movie connection. Virginia Bruce's photo was on "What's the Reason," and an artist drew a graceful girl in a black evening gown to adorn "Object."

Robert Taylor romances Virginia Bruce while I supply the music in *Times Square Lady*. The movie *Society Doctor* had previously established the Taylor-Bruce couple as a box office success.

The publicity crew kept busy adding gimmicks almost daily. One afternoon I received a call to meet with them. When I arrived in the press chief's office, I asked, "Well, boys, what tricks are you up to now?"

"We have a few new ideas," admitted the head brainstormer. "How about an essay contest on the subject 'My Most Vivid Recollection of Times Square'? Then we'll send roving photographers through theater crowds. We'll snap a lot of photos, ostensibly looking for the Times Square Lady."

I noted, "Sounds like more hoopla and folderol."

"Exactly," he chuckled. "While we're at it, we thought we'd sponsor Pinky Tomlin imitation nights. Local versions of amateur hour. Find someone who can do a takeoff of your singing style—if that's possible."

"That sounds OK with me. It'll mean more folks singing and listening to my music." I thought of my hometown friends trying to do imitations. "Wow, I'd love to see the bunch who'll attempt it in Durant, Oklahoma."

"You will."

"What? Don't kid me. I haven't had time to buy a suit of clothes in the last six months, much less take off on a vacation home."

"Then hang onto your hat, Pinky. You're Oklahoma-bound."

I stood there, incredulous, not suspecting what they had in mind.

Finally the publicity chief burst out laughing, congratulating himself on his brilliant plan. "Pinky, we're going to premiere this film in your hometown, Durant. In mid-March you, Robert Taylor, and the whole entourage are going to descend on Oklahoma and light it up like the corner of Hollywood and Vine."

After I recovered from the initial marvelous shock, I began to feel as warm as if the studio had given me a Christmas present. I was going home—*in style*! Only six months after I'd kissed my mother good-bye and climbed in a Model A jalopy, I was heading back as a shining example of poor-boy-makes-good. The only remark I could come up with was, "Sure seems like a lot of fuss."

The publicity man drawled, "Oh, no doubt about it, Pinky. You walked off with that movie. Yep, tucked it under that gangling arm of yours and walked right off with it."

I knew publicity crews were hired to shovel words, and so I didn't let the flack go to my head. But as a Roman philosopher once said, "I much prefer a compliment, insincere or not, to sincere criticism." In any event I was thrilled at the idea of going back to Durant to premiere *Times Square Lady*. I gave a soft whistle as I left the publicity offices. I'd done nothing but work during the time I'd been in California. A visit home, even for a premiere, ought to prove downright restful.

During preparations for the March premiere, the studio gave me the rising-star buildup. I was interviewed for fan magazines, newspapers and MGM's own house bulletin. Once I made the truthful comment to an interviewer, "I really don't know what this is all about." Another reporter asked me for my philosophy of acting. "Philosophy?" I questioned. "I haven't done any real acting. I merely respond to the camera directions and lighting." Then I remembered what Gary Cooper had said about acting and borrowed his lines. "Find out what people expect from your type of character and then give them what they want. That way an actor never seems unnatural or affected, no matter what role he plays."

Besides doing the interviews the studio wanted, I made some other preparations for my trip back to Durant. By my hometown's standards I was now making big money. For the six months of work at the Biltmore, Paramount, and MGM I'd received good salaries. In those days there was no social security tax and almost no income tax. I'd saved nearly everything that I'd made because working back-to-back performances gave me no time to play around. I wore my one good-luck blue suit for every performance at the Paramount, rode the seven-cent streetcar to and from work, and lived in an apartment that would be modest by Oklahoma standards and was excruciatingly cozy by California standards.

Before I left for Oklahoma, I went to the bank and obtained a cashier's check for $35,000. I intended to buy a house for my mother, open a bank account for her in Durant, and see what I could do to get my brothers out of their normal financial jams. When I packed to head home, I was still toting my battered old suitcase, but now I had a $35,000 certified check in the lining.

The big event was scheduled for March 16, 1935—an uptown Saturday night for Durant, Oklahoma. MGM booked the Ritz Theatre and pulled out all the publicity stops, sensing a lot of interest in my return home and perhaps more than a common amount of envy. More than once I heard the remark, "If ole Pink can make it big in Hollywood, let's all pack up and head for California."

I don't automatically hold grudges, but time had not healed all the wounds that had inflicted on me while I was growing up. I remembered the banker refusing me the fifty-dollar loan I needed to cover my father's funeral expenses. I still rankled when I thought of Mr. Swinney telling me that "college jelly beans don't know how to work." I've always agreed with Harry Truman's philosophy: "If someone throws a brick at me, I can catch it and throw it back." The check in my suitcase was the heftiest brick I'd need.

Things had turned out well for me in a spectacularly short time, and I was appropriately humble. I honestly believed in the land-of-opportunity tag pinned to America's lapels. My experience in California had only reinforced my dreams not altered them. Humility is not the same as being a doormat for other people, however. It would be hypocritical for me to claim I had no talent, but it took more than the gift to climb the ladder of success in the Depression. It took a certain kind of courage to act when sixteen million other able-bodied men were on the relief rolls. The money I was able to take back to Durant was truly fruit of my labors and, yes, I was indeed proud of that check.

When I returned home, the Durant newspaper that had sent me off six months previously with only one line on the back page now welcomed me with a full one-page insert. The *Daily Democrat* printed my life story and put up signs pointing out where I had lived. Storefronts held posters and banners, and "Welcome home, Pinky" signs were in abundance.

Metro-Goldwyn-Mayer furnished the biggest automobile they had in their fleet—a twelve-cylinder Packard. Boy, did I return home in style! The theater roped off a special section, and I was allowed to invite fifty friends, all of whom were to be chauffeured to the movie in the impressive automobile. I'm certain that the guests, mostly my mother's Sunday-school friends, were more startled by the car than impressed by me. These ladies put on their white gloves and go-to-meetin' best and climbed in the Packard. They seemed to enjoy the occasion, yet for them there was a slight touch of sin about going to the movies. Durant was a deep Southern Baptist stronghold, and films were a morally gray area along with other "thou shalt nots," such as drinking, card playing, smoking, and dancing. For the gala premiere my mother and her friends overcame their prejudices toward Hollywood fare. Even the Baptist preacher showed up at the Ritz, sitting lowered in his seat as if unsure whether he wanted to be seen.

There were other movieland props besides the car. MGM sent a newsreel camera, a chorus of young starlets, a personal chauffeur for the Packard, and handsome Robert Taylor.

The minute we arrived, I realized there would be trouble about the black driver, Allan Gant. He was a fine young man who worked for the studio and was used to accompanying crews and stars all over the country. Durant, in 1935, still held to many beliefs of the Old South, including the prejudice that the town should stay all-white. Blacks who worked in Durant had to live a few miles south in the all-Negro community Colbert. Durant even had one of the South's infamous signs at the edge of town warning blacks, "Don't let the sun set on you here." Perhaps my hometown was no worse than other small towns of Little Dixie, but it seemed time to change. I called the newspaper and told the editor, "If Allan Gant can't stay in the town, I can't either."

Thoreau is credited with the line, "It's never too late to give up your prejudices." To Durant's credit, the sign at the edge of town was taken down and never put back up. Allan Gant found accommodations at the only decent hotel in town, the Bryan. His stay in town wasn't marred by any trace of unpleasantness. Perhaps all this seems remote now, but it was definitely part of a thankfully bygone era. To put things in perspective, you have to remember that it was 1939 before Hattie McDaniel was honored with a supporting-actress Oscar for her role in *Gone With the Wind*. Before that, blacks had never even been nominated for Academy Awards.

Another force for kindness on our trip to Oklahoma was Robert

In this nightclub scene from *Times Square Lady*, the attention of Virginia Bruce is directed to me. This turn of events doesn't set well with jilted dates Isabel Jewell and Robert Taylor.

Taylor. He was considerate of everyone, especially the "little old ladies" who flocked around him, asking for autographs and hand-shakes. In real life Taylor lived up to his handsome, romantic image. At the time we filmed *Times Square Lady*, Taylor was involved with Irene Hervey. Later he married Barbara Stanwyck. After their divorce he wed Ursula Thiess in 1951. It was the dashing Robert Taylor who planted the first screen kiss on Elizabeth Taylor in 1945.

During our work on the movie Bob and I had double-dated a few times. The studios encouraged film stars to date, often arranging outings if no mutual interest occurred naturally. Bob would take Irene Hervey, and I escorted Virginia Bruce. This was the period when Bob was drawing the standard contract-player salary of $150 a week, while I was making $1,000 a week. He owned a worn-out Plymouth coupé. I didn't own a car, but the studio made the lim-ousine and chauffeur available. We took advantage of MGM's largesse when we wanted to make a night on the town.

Bob confided to me, "Pinky, I've got real money problems. Here I am, breaking into pictures, and people are starting to think of me as a movie star. I'm a long way short of being able to afford the right clothes, car, and house. It's strapping me just to go out on dates."

I felt that Bob was destined for great things in his career. After watching the daily rushes of *Times Square Lady*, I figured that Bob would be in the front ranks of films and finances for many years. I teased him. "I'll make a deal with you, Bob. Three years from today I'll trade bank accounts with you."

"It's a deal," he said, without a second thought. "But you'll be the loser, Pinky."

I could see him mentally totaling the difference in our current sal-aries, but I proved a better fortune-teller than he. After *Times Square Lady* proved successful, Universal Studios borrowed Bob for a starring role in *Magnificent Obsession*. That film turned out so well that MGM exercised its option on his services at the lifetime rate of a minimum $3,500 a week.

In March, 1935, however, Bob considered himself a hardship case. I consoled him with my sad story of being too busy to spend any of the money I'd made. "I have most of it right here to put in the bank."

A posed publicity photograph of me with Irene Hervey. In the mid-thirties, Irene was the real life object of Robert Taylor's affections and we would often doubledate.

"You ought to throw yourself a party, Pinky. Blow a little on yourself."

"I'd rather be an exception to that old show-business rule—they spend it when they have it, and they spend it when they don't."

My brothers, Walter and Troy, came by as Bob and I were having this financial discussion. After listening awhile, Troy asked, "Exactly what are you going to do with that check?"

I grinned at my brother, who had grown to be the family tall man at six feet, four inches. "Don't get any ideas about that money, High Pockets. You already heard me say that check buys Mom a house."

He cued me in on some local politics. "Did you know that bankers from both banks on Main Street are trying every trick in the book to get that money on deposit in their bank? You-know-who is having a fit hoping you'll show up on his doorstep."

"Wonderful!" I cried, delighted that he was finally going to put out the welcome mat for me.

"Wonderful?" asked Troy, who knew there was no love lost between me and the banker. "Pinky, that California sun must have baked your brain about the same silly color as your hair."

I ignored the brotherly insult. "Come on, kid. We've got to pay a call on him. I want to present this check to him for personal deposit."

We marched to downtown Durant with Walter and Troy staring in disbelief. I went up to the red-brick edifice. As I opened the glass front door, things seemed to move into slow motion. The banker himself came sliding forward to greet me, grinning and pumping my arm in a hefty handshake. "My boy, my boy, I knew all along you'd make it."

The customers in the bank gathered around, sharing the excitement, asking for autographs, watching our financial transactions. Everyone was cordial, including me to the banker. I placed the check on deposit in his bank and left.

Promptly at the opening of business the next morning, I went back to the bank. I was the first customer waiting to see him. Speaking softly, I told him cordially, "I'd like to withdraw my money."

He turned pale, looked in all directions as if to spot robbers, and then stammered, "But, why? Oh, Pinky, my boy, you don't mean that. You want it all back?"

"Yes, sir. Right now."

He mopped his forehead with a handkerchief, even though the morning was chilly. "Right now? All of it?"

Again I agreed. "Yes, sir. All of it. Right this very minute."

"Why?" he groaned.

Actually there were many reasons behind my request. They were connected with growing up poor in a town controlled by a few rich men. But the primary reason was more explicit.

"Last year I came here and asked to borrow fifty dollars to pay my father's funeral expenses. Your words then—and I quote—were, 'No collateral, no loan.'"

He pleaded, "But that was bank policy!"

"I have a policy about money, too—now that I have some of my own. If you can't trust me for fifty, I certainly can't trust you with thirty-five thousand."

I felt as vindicated as if I'd climbed Mount Everest. He had to retrieve the check from the Dallas clearinghouse. He returned it to me without a word. He also had to take an embarrassing sign out of the front window of his bank. In those days state-controlled banks had to post the capital and surplus deposits of their institution. In this case, the bank had posted, "Capital—$45,000. Surplus—$35,000."

After this incident I took the check across the street and deposited it without fanfare at the competing bank. I figured that that particular score was even.

I then turned my attention to the premiere. The Ritz theatre was decked and draped for the evening's big showing. The film went over well with my hometown family and friends. After the movie was shown, I stepped onstage and made some brief remarks—basically, "Thanks for coming." Afterwards we delivered my mother and her friends back to their homes by Packard. As we passed some of the familiar town landmarks, I spotted Swinney's Drugstore. Again I remembered the druggist's remark about "college jelly beans" and their inability to hold a job. I also remembered my boastful remark of a few summers ago—that I'd come back to town in a car so big I'd have to circle the block just to park. Now was my chance. I leaned over and tapped chauffeur Allan Gant. "Go down to the next stop sign, circle the block, and pull up in front of Swinney's Drug. When we get there, tap your horn. Don't tap it easy, either."

Allan grinned, sensing some fun. He loved to drive that Packard and took care of it as if it were his own. When he pulled curbside, he laid into the horn full blast, flashed the lights, and hollered for curb service. My mother and her cronies in the back seat looked shocked. I was perched on an extra jumpseat in the middle of the car, enjoying every moment.

The druggist came out, laughed, and shook his head. I believe he was nearly as happy as I that I'd made my prophesy come true. "I'm tickled to death for you, Pinky," he said, and then provided curb service for everyone.

I was glad to settle old scores, but I was the first to admit that luck, timing, and being in the right places had certainly helped my career. I was indeed fortunate in having my success come so fast. Both fame and luck can be fleeting. Fred Allen once quipped, "A celebrity is a person who works hard all his life to become well known, then wears dark glasses to avoid being recognized." I wasn't in the sunglasses-disguise stage and hoped I never would be. I knew that, come Monday morning, I'd have to go back to California and continue the hard-working routines that had given me this opportunity. But I savored every last minute of my return to Durant, basking in the glory of my personal Horatio Alger story.

13

Star-building'

The year 1935 brought a lot of firsts. The first Mother of the Year was selected in Gainesville, Georgia. The first beer was sold in cans. The first Social Security Act passed Congress. Oklahoma City installed the first parking meters. For me, 1935 was the first year I specialized in one area of show business. The time had come to make a decision. I couldn't go on cutting up my career among films, radio, nightclubs, theaters, records, and personal appearances.

The movie industry went through a siege of growing pains in the mid-thirties. Giant consolidated studios rose from the debris of many smaller ones. The mergers were the result of warfare rather than peaceful acquisition. In 1935 alone, Republic managed to cannibalize Imperial, Majestic, Mascot, Monogram, and Liberty film companies. The big-name studios emerged and held tremendous power. Paramount, RKO, Columbia, Universal, Twentieth Century Fox, and MGM ruled Hollywood.

From these conglomerates emerged another facet of big-time entertainment—the star-building system. I had this program explained to me by Lucien Hubbard after we finished filming *Times Square Lady*. He told me, "Pinky, we've got a spot for you in the star-building system."

"What's involved? Acting and singing lessons? Remember, you told me simply to 'act natural' for my first film."

"Sure, but normally we send prospective contract players to school. It works out well. We expect to get some big stars out of students such as Judy Garland, Donald O'Connor, Betty Grable, and Robert Taylor."

"I know Taylor is headed for great things," I plugged my friend. "But I don't know about me. How much time does star school take?" "Twenty-five hours a day, eight days a week," he laughed. "You take singing, acting, dancing, exercise, speech, acrobatic lessons— the works. We get an option on your services when you finish."

"What kind of salary would I get? MGM's paying me a thousand a week right now."

"You'd get the standard contract at a hundred and fifty a week."

"Whoops, that'd mean quite a salary cut," I blurted. "I've been making a thousand here and another twelve hundred at the Paramount. I'm not sure I can afford to be a star."

I asked for some time to think things over. There were obvious advantages to the star-building school. It would allow me to do roles outside the homey, bashful country-boy typecasting. They'd try me in different wardrobes and makeups until they found a winning combination. On the negative side, I might be lost in the shuffle of talented players. Not everyone was going to emerge as successfully as Alice Faye, Clark Gable, Deanna Durbin, and the others Hubbard had mentioned.

After thinking it over and discussing it with some of my friends, I decided not to sacrifice my established earning power as a headliner for the unguaranteed chance at movie stardom. Another factor was that, if I went the film route, I'd be restricted in the amount of time I could devote to my music. I thought about the hit songs of 1935— "You Are My Lucky Star," "The Music Goes Round and Round," and "Moon over Miami." I believed that I had some hit songs lurking in my brain too. My name was pretty well known in music circles now. The time was right to promote my own songs.

I met again with MGM executives and turned down the star-school offer. They upped the ante to five hundred a week, but I declined, saying, "Twenty-six weeks is too long at this point in my life." Perhaps I made a big mistake, but it certainly seemed right at the time.

After declining the chance to go to film school, I realized that I wouldn't get any extra help with my acting. I'd have to do roles that called for a country hayseed with a slight twist of corny romance.

During *Times Square Lady*, MGM had sent me to Josephine Dillon for help on particular scenes. Dillon, who was Mrs. Clark Gable at the time, had her own speech school. She worked with many up-and-coming actors, including Clark. She was an excellent coach, and among those in the know she was given major credit in turning Gable into a star. She taught him to play up his he-man image. After a while Gable began to believe in his image and dropped Josephine for someone younger and flashier. I certainly profited from studying with Dillon. I worked with her subsequently, and she became a good friend to my whole family.

While I was still at MGM, the studio rewarded me for the success of *Times Square Lady* by providing a chauffeured limousine and a suite of rooms at the Ambassador Hotel. When old friends came to visit me, I was able to put them up at the Ambassador. The hotel was a favorite with show-business people. In 1927 some folks had gathered at the Ambassador to discuss the idea of awards for movies. They doodled rough sketches of possible statues to be awarded. The ultimate design for the Oscar came from Cedric Gibbon—a penciled sketch on an Ambassador tablecloth.

Two visitors who came to see me in 1935 were Eddie and Wilma Chiles. They were old college friends who arrived in a beat-up Plymouth roadster. They were typical tourists, eager to see the sights. I put them up at the Ambassador and promised them a good time, relying on the limousine to get us around.

Eddie Chiles's credentials in 1935 weren't too impressive, but his dreams were. He put his net worth at "one truck and fifty feet of oil-well casing." His plans were bigger. He intended to build a worldwide well-servicing organization. He already had the name picked out: the Western Company of North America. His assets just didn't match his ambitions in 1935.

Eddie, Wilma, and I made the grand tour of show-business night spots, including the Trocadero, Romanoff's, the Mocambo, and several illegal gambling spots. We spent one evening at the Palomar Dance Palace, at Third and Vermont in Los Angeles. I knew that the Casa Loma Orchestra was appearing there, and I was looking forward to seeing my old friend Grady Watts. Grady had telephoned me, told me the orchestra had a good arrangement of "The Object of My Affection," and hoped I'd stop by to hear it.

I laughed. "Grady, you didn't think too much of my song when I came to Chicago a couple of years ago. Remember when I tried to give you half interest in it?"

He joined the humor. "Hey, let bygones be bygones, will you?" Again he invited me to drop by and hear the Casa Loma Orchestra. "We'll even let you sing your song," he promised.

What an invitation! That night when we arrived at the Palomar, I went over to shake hands with Grady. When he saw me coming, he abruptly turned his back. Then he bent over, yanked up his coattail and said, "Give me the swift kick I deserve for turning down a half interest in 'Object!'"

This unorthodox greeting became standard between us whenever we met from then on. Grady never forgot his mistake about the song. On the other hand, I was forever grateful that I hadn't succeeded in giving away half interest in my lifetime meal ticket.

Another famous nightclub on Sunset Boulevard, or the Strip as it was known locally, was the Trocadero. Nat King Cole was the featured performer. He held forth in the King Cole Room, and his hit song at the time was "Straighten Up and Fly Right." On Sunday nights the Trocadero featured new talent. Milton Berle, Jack Benny, Rudy Vallee, Eddie Cantor, and other big names took turns as master of ceremonies, presenting "discoveries." I had a turn at the Trocadero and had the pleasure of introducing a young lady recently arrived from Texas. She had an act that featured singing swing arrangements of operatic arias. Her outstanding performance that night was a lively version of the air from *Martha*. Later she switched to musical comedies. Everyone remembers Mary Martin and her wonderful success in such hits as *South Pacific*, *The Sound of Music*, and *Peter Pan*.

While Eddie and Wilma Chiles were in Los Angeles, I took them to the Cocoanut Grove. This club was the current "in" place, usually overflowing with celebrities. The food at the Grove was good, the music mellow, and the atmosphere free of autograph hunters. Show people weren't bothered unless they arranged it themselves. The place was always jammed. Evidently stars felt there was safety in numbers.

The music at the Cocoanut Grove was provided by such pros as Eddie Duchin, Guy Lombardo, and Freddie Martin. When I happened to be in the audience, I was usually recognized and asked to sing a few numbers. Normally I'd oblige. In all honesty I can say that I never tired of performing "The Object of My Affection." Forty-seven years after writing it, I still get a thrill whenever I hear it played.

During the hectic years of folderol about movie stars, autograph seekers plagued many entertainment people. The question of privacy was always ticklish. The best solution was offered by Bing Crosby. He was constantly surrounded by fans. He always smiled and accommodated them graciously. Once I asked him if he was bothered by all the scratching and scrawling on napkins and matchbooks.

"Nope," he said quickly. "Not a bit."

"Seems like a lot of inconvenience," I said. "Don't you think you're entitled to a night out with no strings attached?"

Bing gave me one of his famous cockeyed smiles and a mischievous tilt of his head. "Before I leave home I take a good look in the mirror. I say to myself, 'Look here, you character. Those fans out there put you where you are. Without them you'd be a fat zero so don't forget them.'"

I thought Bing's attitude was refreshing. How different from the story told of Norma Talmadge, who after her retirement told autograph hunters, "Go away, I don't need you anymore."

Every star had his own opinion on what invaded his privacy. I thought highly of Humphrey Bogart's belief that "the only thing you owe the public is a good performance," but it was hard to quibble with Bing Crosby's advice, "If you don't want to be recognized, stay home." This commonsense attitude typified Crosby. He was a man of humility, kindness, and deep convictions, a sensitive performer and a sensible human being.

One evening I told Bing about my college-days crush on his costar Mary Brian. "I always enjoyed your movies, Bing, but the real attraction was Mary. She is sure one beautiful girl."

"You ought to call her up and get a date," he drawled.

I was enough of a country boy to turn double pink at the suggestion. "She'd laugh me out of town," I worried.

"I doubt it. She's been to see you at the Biltmore Bowl. Heck, where's your courage, kid?"

"Back home in the south forty!" But I resolved to call Mary Brian as soon as I could work up the nerve. My social life wasn't extensive; it was curtailed effectively by back-to-back appearances at the Biltmore and the Paramount. Apart from the promotional dates arranged for me with Virginia Bruce, I really had neither the time nor the inclination to go out. Part of the reason was the young lady back in Oklahoma with whom I still kept in touch by letter and phone and whom I had seen on a few occasions. Joanne Alcorn was still a student at the University of Oklahoma, but I hadn't forgotten her by any means. I imagined myself still waiting for her to grow up. During my year in California I had met some cute starlets—Jean Parker, Betty Grable, and Alice Faye—but it seemed to me that Oklahoma girls compared rather well.

I talked to Wilma Chiles about my lingering affection for Joanne Alcorn. Wilma and Joanne were sorority sisters. I asked Wilma casually, "Say, is Joanne going with anyone in particular these days?"

Wilma saw right through me. She reassured me by saying, "Oh, I think the object of Joanne's affection is still pink."

I felt much better. We continued our tour of Hollywood's entertainment meccas. At the end of the week we discovered that their Plymouth roadster had not fared well in the Ambassador parking lot. The old coupé had developed three flat tires and a broken starter cable. Eddie was horrified. "How am I going to fix that blasted thing? My wallet's as flat as those tires."

I contributed four tires, a garage mechanic, and five hundred dollars to the unfortunate situation. Eddie promised to pay me back. I didn't doubt it, knowing he was a man of hard work and a man of his word.

Over the next year I received checks from Texas in amounts of fifty and sixty dollars until every penny was repaid. During that year Eddie Chiles also increased his oil-field assets to two trucks and one hundred feet of well casing. Today, of course, he is president and chairman of the board of the Western Company of North America. His firm constructs and delivers the huge offshore drilling rigs. Western's technology is in use all over the world, pioneering important advances in the energy field. To me Eddie Chiles remains a cherished friend, partly because we both started out with more dreams than assets.

14

Moviemaking

I scrambled among movie sets at three different studios during the rest of 1935 and 1936–1937. *King Solomon of Broadway* was filmed at Universal, *Smart Girl* at Walter Wanger Productions, and four independents at Maurice Conn studios. For the four musicals at Maurice Conn I not only appeared as an actor but also wrote and scored the music.

Music in all these films ran the gamut from Broadway-type production numbers down to one man and a guitar. Usually I sang my songs to the leading lady using a nightclub backdrop. Film scripts were always pressed to find ways to work in songs. Sometimes the setting was farfetched, but a musical of that era was expected to combine vaudeville, the Ziegfeld Follies, square dances, and serenades. In one film I burst into song in the middle of a department store.

None of these films was particularly original. Movies in the midthirties imitated each other shamelessly. Once a "trend" was imagined, every studio rushed to grind out that kind of movie. Stories, stars, and titles copied each other. There were a half-dozen films titled, *In Old* ————, and the customer could fill in the blank with Oklahoma, Arizona, Kentucky, Wyoming, Santa Fe, or San Antonio. Hollywood mass-produced *Down in* ———— films, too, and another brand of *Home in* ———— titles. Many of these pictures were semi-westerns. Square-dance calls were a popular, standard feature. Gene Autry did the first number in 1934's *In Old Santa Fe.* They were still going strong in 1952, when I was the square-dance caller in *The Story of Will Rogers.*

The imitative titles didn't bother the audience. It didn't worry

100

A production number from *With Love and Kisses*. Toby Wing is in front of me and she is gazing at famous restaurateur Michael Romanoff.

anyone that the title sometimes had little to do with the plot. *Round Up Time in Texas* turned out to be about African tribesmen. *King Solomon of Broadway* lumped the Bible with Manhattan. "The Phantom Empire" on radio had a storyline in which a radio announcer fell through a dude-ranch cave into an underground kingdom. It helps to remember that films were competing with such popular entertainment as Clyde Beatty's animal acts, Saturday-morning radio serials, and "Our Gang" comedies.

King Solomon of Broadway had an average storyline, and I had an above-average part that consisted largely of supporting veteran actor Edmund Lowe. I reported to the Universal lot in June, 1935. They promptly dubbed me "the wonder boy." That made me wonder. The *Hollywood Reporter* insisted once again that I was "good ole Pink, the bashful, lovable, farmer boy from Oklahoma."

The cast also included Dorothy Page, Ed Pawley, and Lewis Henry. I wrote and sang the novelty song, "That's What You Think." Again I considered it a lucky break to perform my own material. During this era most studios retained resident teams of songwriters. Warner Brothers had Dubin and Warren, and Paramount kept Robbins and Rainger in their stable. Some of the other big names scoring for the movies included Cole Porter, Rodgers and Hart, the Gershwins, Jerome Kern, and Johnny Mercer. For lyrics I believe the all-time boss of us all was Johnny Mercer. For melodies my all-time favorites were Sammie Fain ("Love Is a Many-splendored Thing") and Henry Mancini's many hits, including "Moon River."

Musically the thirties were interesting times. A hit would become such a solid favorite that every band and singer would make it part of their permanent repertoire. Audiences willingly heard these melodies over and over, making them part of their lives. Even today men and women come up to tell me how they associate certain songs I wrote with distinct phases of their younger days, how they danced to special melodies, fell in love, and still claim particular music as "our song."

It was easy to get attached to songs that stayed around a long time, unlike today, when a number must make it quickly or be discarded on the charts. One thing that helped was that there were only a few songwriters. A "hit" did not have to depend on gaining quick air

102

I'm sitting pretty as *King Solomon of Broadway*, surrounded by Universal Studio starlets.

time, having acres of backup guitars, or providing a built-in light-and-sound show. In my opinion, massive amplification has been an assault on American music. We now have too many songs played too loudly without lyrics that can be heard or remembered. If this sounds like sour grapes, blame it on sour music.

Besides telling me they have enjoyed my music through the years, fans usually ask me, "How do you write a song?" I usually tell them the simplest way is to find a catchy title and then build a musical story to fit it. I think titles serve as window dressing for a song. A title should make people pick up the sheet music or record and look at it—then buy it. Once I developed a terrific title but was never able to find the musical story to go with it (to this day I haven't completed, "Please Don't Say Please Don't"). Other titles worked out easier—"Object" from a lawbook, "Love Bug" from a folksaying, and "I Told Santa Claus to Bring Me You" from the holiday trade.

For *King Solomon of Broadway* I wrote the songs "That's What You Think" and "The Trouble With Me Is You." The word *you* pops up in my titles far more often than the pronoun *I*. This isn't simply a ploy to gain audience reaction and empathy. Entertainers, by their basic desire to be onstage, harbor strong egos. They must battle constantly to keep their vanity in check by personal self-knowledge of their limitations and human shortcomings. Lucille Harper's deadly accurate quip, "One nice thing about egotists: they don't talk about other people," is only too true in show business. Entertainers end up making public confessions that shouldn't be made, reveal private traumas when they needn't subject themselves to such scrutiny, and fall over the thin line that divides public performer from private person. Personalities who cannot, or will not, make this distinction inevitably suffer. P. T. Barnum and Hollywood led many performers to believe that you can fool all of the people all of the time, but entertainers should never try to fool themselves. Those who read their own press releases and try to lead their private lives for public consumption end up suckers.

The invented publicity was an important part of the movie game in the thirties. The whole idea of films is fiction. Glamour, exciting lives, scandal, and make-believe fit a pattern. Louis B. Mayer, who introduced the star system at Metro, gave forth with the rule that stars must either play the publicity game or hang up their costumes and go home.

King Solomon of Broadway fit right into the traditional mold of dress-up and make-believe. Of course the hero and heroine fell in love, and of course it was forever. My songs were meant to convey this essence of the film. Apparently they succeeded. When we finished the picture, Universal offered me a three-year contract at a thousand dollars a week. Did I sign? Right on the dotted line.

Good reviews and good box-office receipts greeted the movie. I got a lot of fan mail and made the gossip columns. A national fan club was organized, much to my surprise and appreciation.

My next project was *Smart Girl* for Walter Wanger Productions. It starred Ida Lupino and Kent Taylor. Wanger was one of moviemaking's real veterans, having come to California in World War I as an army officer assigned to the Public Information Committee. He'd helped make pro-Army films. Afterwards he stayed on as a civilian, becoming production supervisor at Paramount's Astoria Studios with the advent of talkies in 1928.

Ida Lupino was in her heyday as a sultry starlet. Later she became one of Hollywood's accomplished but rare woman directors. She showed her talent with sensitive directing in such stories as *Young Lovers* (1950), about a young dancer affected by polio.

Smart Girl was another success. My mail increased to the point that I had to hire a secretary. She tried to answer some of the letters and send out the autographed pictures the fans asked for. The most common questions in the letters were, "Are you married?" and "I've written a great song. Will you look at it?" There were quite a few requests for money too. The most amazing fan letter I ever received was from a woman in Iowa who insisted she'd had my baby by immaculate conception.

After *Smart Girl* I went to Maurice Conn productions for the rest of 1936–37. The four independent musicals were titled, *Swing It, Professor*, *Thanks for Listenin'*, *With Love and Kisses*, and *Sing While You're Able*. They were interesting to me because I got the chance to do the musical scoring. All four were released in 1937–38.

On the set of *With Love and Kisses*, I worked with director Marshall Neilan, whose nickname was Mickey. He had been one of Mary Pickford's directors in earlier days. By the end of the thirties, Mickey had fallen on hard times, drinking heavily and working at odd film jobs. After finishing the series of musicals, he never directed again. His drinking caused no problem for us on the sets. Most of the time he used a coffee cup to disguise his imbibing.

My basic role was to do shy comedy and sing my songs. Mickey Neilan and I shared some interesting conversations. He typified to me the terrible ups and downs that often plague an entertainer's life. Yes, he believed in high living at the Cocoanut Grove, sometimes on borrowed cash. But he also believed in hard work and not wasting time in front of the cameras. He was forty-six at the time we made *With Love and Kisses*. It would be another twenty years before he died of alcoholism and cancer in a charity hospital. But even in 1937 he sensed that the road lay downhill. He once remarked, "I had the misfortune to believe in bad booze and good times." Despite a reported gratuity of five hundred dollars a week from Mary Pickford, Neilan seemed on hard times financially. He told me, "Some weeks I used to make fifteen thousand, now I can't get fifteen cents."

A lot of Neilan's problems stemmed from his own immense creativity. Colleen Moore, one of the stars he helped develop, commented, "Mickey was a genius who didn't grow up until it was too late." He was also arrogant with the studio heads, behavior that got him thrown off a lot of properties. One of his famous wisecracks that made him persona non grata was, "An empty taxicab drove up and Louis B. Mayer got out."

Mickey's troubles didn't interfere with our film work. We came in on time and under budget.

During the time I was working on the independent musicals, my mother came to California to visit me. She really came out to check up on me and to make sure I hadn't fallen into any of the evils of Hollywood life. She was surprised at how much hard work went into making a movie. She was even more shocked at the beautiful California countryside. Of course, I didn't take my mother to the nightspots or gambling dens. Instead we drove through the hills and orange orchards, along the coast, and down to the shore. She remarked, "God spent six days making the heavens and the earth. Then on the seventh day he must have created California."

I sang seven songs in *With Love and Kisses*, a number that strained the credulity of everyone but the screenwriters. One was done with a nightclub setting. The others were scattered about the countryside. Arthur Houseman, Russell Hopton, Kane Richmond, and Fuzzy Knight appeared in the cast. Other performers had supporting roles in cameo appearances, playing themselves. These included the Peters Sisters, Chelito and Gabriel, Jerry Bergen, and Billy Gray.

My leading lady was Toby Wing, who was once billed as "Hollywood's most perfect chorus girl." She was another of the tall, blonde femme fatale types so popular in the thirties. She was a veteran of the Busby Berkeley musicals at MGM. She'd appeared with Eddie Cantor in *The Kid from Spain* when she was only sixteen years old. At Paramount she'd made *Search for Beauty* and *Murder at the Vanities*.

Virginia Bruce, Mary Brian, and Toby Wing were among the cute up-and-coming starlets of the time. The big-name leading ladies were Myrna Loy, Norma Shearer, Bette Davis, Marion Davies, Joan Crawford, Jean Harlow, and Katharine Hepburn. The box office could count on a film that starred Claudette Colbert, Marlene Dietrich, Irene Dunne, Dorothy Lamour, or Rosalind Russell. That was quite an impressive list of "bankable" female leads, compared to the few who have superstar status today.

Besides Toby Wing, I had another costar in *With Love and Kisses*. This was Minnie—just Minnie, no last name. Minnie was a cow, a cow with one horn. Minnie had her picture on all the window-card posters that were sent to theaters. Minnie's role was fairly important for the story line of this fluff creation. I played a country boy who was unable to sing unless my favorite bovine was by my side. In the movie I sent some of my songs to a New York radio singer, who, villain that he was, introduced the music as his own. I then became infuriated, borrowed train fare from the local sheriff, hightailed it to Broadway, and—wham—was unable to sing without Minnie the cow.

Silly? Yes. Entertaining? Apparently. Moviegoers lined up for this kind of zany musical comedy. The idea of using an animal had been

There were seven musical numbers in *With Love and Kisses*. This one featured me with co-star Toby Wing.

lifted from the enormously successful *State Fair*, starring Will Rogers. In that film a huge hog, Blue Boy, was Will's sidekick. At the end of the filming the studio tried to give the pig to Will, suggesting he fatten it at his ranch and then slaughter it. Will replied, "I could never eat a fellow actor!" Fortunately for me, there was no talk of presenting me with Minnie the cow.

When we remember how successful escapist entertainment was throughout the thirties, it's important to take the times into consideration. The headlines of 1936–37 were "General Motors Turns Off Heat to Cool Down Strike" and "Hauptmann Put to Death for Lindbergh Kidnapping." People sought relief from a world in which Mussolini was seizing Ethiopia and hunger was seizing American stomachs. People lapped up entertainment of any kind. They went crazy over the candid-camera fad. They bought six million copies of the book *Gone with the Wind* in less than six months. They sang "I'm an Old Cowhand" and snapped up Roosevelt's 1936 campaign slogan, "Prosperity is just around the corner."

The press releases for *With Love and Kisses* again insisted, "Pinky's just an old cowhand." Another fabricated press release insisted that "Pinky Tomlin astounds song writing world and never took a music lesson." My twang was called "a menace to the American slanguage" and compared with Jimmy Durante's. Though I'd been in California for nearly four years, one interviewer decided that my drawl was a "holdover from the rural Oklahoma life from which he is less than a year removed." This interviewer invented a quote for me: "I reckin the way they say stuff daown in Okly-homey is good enuff fer me right naow. I mite git eddicated afters awhile, but I don't rightly knaow."

It took considerable finesse by the studios to hide the fact I had a university degree in music and had studied speech with Josephine Dillon.

I had an opportunity to put all my musical training to use in scoring *Swing It, Professor*, *Thanks for Listenin'*, and *Sing While You're Able*. Composing a motion-picture score is more than simply writing suitable background sounds. Screen music was meant to be unobtrusive except during vocal or dance numbers. A composer took into account the general mood of the scene and then built a quiet accompanying

The studio favored "just plain ole' bashful Pink" publicity shots. The hat and glasses were my trademarks along with casual clothes and guitar.

tempo. Scenes change so rapidly on the screen that only a few bars of melody are usually needed. On the other hand, all the scenes need some overall musical unity.

In scoring, sometimes I'd simply sit with my guitar and improvise. This was fairly easy when all I had to provide was mood music. When the storyline needed sound effects, I'd compose melodies to augment the plot. The storylines were often simple, but sometimes the music wasn't.

Dialogue determined how extensive the background music could be. Toby Wing's speaking voice was fairly high-pitched. Mine was somewhat husky. So I had to consider spoken pitch as well as musical pitch. Our voices already had plenty of "color." The music behind them had to be fairly bland.

No one can appreciate what music adds to films unless he sits through a silent screening. A musical comedy, in particular, has to sound like one as well as look like it. A screen composer has a lot more restrictions than a "live" performer. It was good experience for me to score the four musicals, but I didn't intend to take it up as a full-time career.

Original film scoring was only beginning at the time I was doing it. Before the thirties background music was usually an adaptation of a classic. A lot of Debussy and public-domain melodies were heard in the early movies. Later originality became important largely through the work of such composers as Max Steiner, Alfred Newman, Dimitri Tiomkin, and Miklos Rosza. Unfortunately, contemporary film scoring seems to have given up music in favor of noise. A motion picture is now broken down by footage into separate scenes. The exact number of seconds of music required is mathematically calculated by computer. Some of the current dissonance on film might be called sound effects with orchestra. A few such nonmusical scores include those for *In Cold Blood*, *Cool Hand Luke*, and *The Sniper*.

Back in 1937 it didn't bother Maurice Conn Productions that their "uneducated actor who never took a music lesson" could compose and score four films. They simply ignored my duties as composer and went on issuing backwoods background publicity. They were trying

111

In this domestic scene between Toby Wing and me from *With Love and Kisses*, I attempt to teach her the fine art of frying eggs.

to promote me as a successor to Will Rogers, who had been lost in a plane crash the previous year.

I did what I could, within limits, not to destroy my credibility as a country boy. The best lines I ever heard about actors and education came from Hermione Gingold. She said: "I got all the schooling any actress needs. That is, I learned to write enough to sign contracts."

It was considered a star's job to grab both the brass ring of Hollywood's merry-go-round and headlines in the gossip columns. The studios tried to invent a romance between me and leading lady Toby Wing. In those days nearly every man-woman pair who appeared together in movies were romantically linked by the fan magazines. The studios encouraged their stars to be "items" for Louella Parsons. There was some truth in the cliché "The life-span of a matinee idol is three marriages or five years, whichever comes first." It boiled down to the fact that a star could either supply the gossip or have the studio flacks invent it. There were also undercover sources, such as the masseurs, manicurists, and salespeople of Beverly Hills. Medical personnel at the major studios were considered prime confidential sources. Hedda Hopper once claimed that she often knew a girl was pregnant before the girl herself found out.

Hedda Hopper and Louella Parsons built their empires on such trivia. Through the forties they remained about the most important duo in show business. Usually they checked their stories for accuracy—especially if they liked you. No one could question their loyalty to the movie industry. They went to well-publicized lengths to scoop each other's stories, often engaging in public feuds. Louella was famous for abrupt tongue lashings that she delivered to stars who had failed to provide her with exclusive stories. I was lucky that most of the times that my name appeared in print it was complimentary.

15

Hometown Friends

My final picture for Universal was *Don't Get Personal*, with James Dunn and Sally Eilers. Sally had displayed some comic talent in 1928 in *The Goodbye Kiss*, but her role in *Don't Get Personal* was merely cutesy. James Dunn came to the set straight from *The Pay Off* at Warners. *Don't Get Personal* was only one of a string of "don't" movies that included *Don't Ever Marry*, *Don't Bet on Blondes*, and *Don't Monkey with the Buzz Saw*.

When filming finished, I went to Durant for a family visit. I enjoyed seeing such old friends as Bennett Story, editor of the paper; Fenton ("Duke") Taylor, with whom I'd played ball in high school; and Lynn Abbott, the guy who had driven the car to Ponca City the night I'd been composing "The Object of My Affection."

Bennett Story, being a newspaperman, kept up with what was going on all over the Southwest. He remarked, "Pinky, one of your old friends is down at the Baker Hotel in Dallas this week."

"Who's that?" I asked.

"Herbie Kay. His orchestra, too."

"Herbie Kay? Sure, he's a good friend, but if his orchestra is appearing at the Baker, I've got real connections. My former accompanist and long-time buddy, Claude Kennedy, plays piano for Herbie." I went on to tell the story of how I had "loaned" Claude to Herbie at the Cocoanut Grove. I had a lot of fond memories of Claude. After a little reminiscing, I said impulsively, "Let's pile in the car and go see the show at the Baker."

Five of us—Bennett Story, Lynn Abbott, Duke Taylor, my brother Troy, and I—made a quick trip south of the Red River. At the Baker I arranged for a large table near the band, hoping we could surprise Herbie and Claude. They were too busy performing to see me, so after a while I sent a note to the bandstand. It was wonderful seeing Claude again. Herbie Kay graciously invited me to the stage and asked me to do a few numbers "off the cuff."

There was applause for my impromptu appearance. As I trooped onstage I was smiling to myself at the idea that this was truly "off the cuff." Claude had helped me work out the original arrangement of "Object" in 1934. He knew almost all my material by memory, had gone with me to my screen test at MGM, and had accompanied me thousands of times. So this off-the-cuff performance might be spontaneous, but it was hardly unrehearsed.

The audience bought the idea, however, and responded generously with applause. For me the big thrill was performing in front of my hometown friends.

A few days later Bennett Story wrote a column for the Durant paper in which he told about our trip. He said several nice things about our outing to Dallas, but the most important phrase was that he said that my performance was truly professional. Sure it's nice to be praised in your hometown—*especially* in your hometown—but the words "full fledged songwriter and mature performer" pleased me even more.

I wasn't naïve to the point of suspecting that Durant would suddenly revere me as a native son. I still believed, talented or not, that if I'd lived my whole life in Bryan County I might well have starved to death. There had been no magic formulas for the success I'd had, lucky breaks and good timing notwithstanding. I've always cherished my mother's tart line, "Yes, it's amazing that the harder Pinky works the luckier he gets."

It's difficult for many younger Americans to realize what a stopper the Depression years put on progress. People who wanted to succeed in that era had to have an abnormal amount of determination. Drive, tenacity, and ambition were essential. Thousands of families picked up stakes and traveled U.S. 66 in search of something better than their lives on the used-up farmlands. It remains a black mark on America's social conscience that these people were labeled ignorant and unwilling to work.

115

I suppose progress was being made in 1936–37, but not much of it was people progress. Octane aviation gas was invented, Boulder Dam was completed, the DC-3 was introduced to the skies, and the Triborough Bridge was built in New York City. But all across America families had to flee for their lives to avoid starvation. This period of history still fascinates and infuriates me. It was a time when life expectancy was only fifty-nine years, a time when people who exercised their right to the pursuit of happiness were derided with the tag "Okie." The song "Don't Blame Me" went to the top of the hit-parade charts, and it seemed to me to typify the whole country's attitude toward my home state.

16

Headliner at the Roxy

New York City—I'd heard the names of the famous landmarks but had never seen them—Times Square, the Empire State Building, Broadway, the Roxy Theatre. In February, 1936, I got my first glimpse of the city as it lay under a cloak of snow and fog. I was booked for a two-week run as headliner at the Roxy.

The stage show tried to give the customer the works. Tickets cost a quarter in the afternoon and forty cents after six. The audience watched a show that included a house orchestra, lines of dancing girls, a newsreel, a first-run movie, and an "in-person" star act.

The vaudeville show of the twenties had given way to the headliner acts of the thirties. High-kicking chorus lines were standard. Stage shows were elaborate "presentations." Some theaters placed the orchestra onstage; others wired the bandstands electrically so that the entire stage could be moved up, down, or back to make room for the various acts.

Headlining was rewarding, yet it was hard work—and lonely. The beauty of a stage show was that people came hoping to be entertained. The orchestra in the pit and the spotlight on me never failed to give me a thrill and a case of the shivers. It's a naked feeling: you're the only ace on the poker table.

Live performances are unpredictable. One audience will love you; another will turn a deaf ear. Audiences, like entertainers, can be up, down, tired, out of sorts, cold, or lazy. The burden is squarely on the performer. He must shake up an audience, snap them out of their doldrums, wake them, and warm them. This demands true communication. Never can you simply walk out and expect to mumble until things begin to click. I always wrote into my contracts that I'd be given a minimum of one-and-a-half hours of rehearsal time before the first performance. Many staff band conductors would try to shorten the time, saying, "Aw, the first performance is really a run-through anyway."

"Not for me," I'd reply. "Besides, the first show is the one the critics catch."

When a house bandleader would mess up a number in rehearsal and then try to slide by with saying, "OK, what's next?" I'd reply curtly, "This same number is next—until we get it right."

I never went before an audience unprepared. I had more respect for people who had paid money to see me than to walk out and wander around wondering what to do next. If you've been hired to entertain, you'd better come on strong.

My in-person act at the Roxy had followed the booking of the movie *Don't Get Personal*. As a result, I arrived in New York to warm audiences. The movie had primed their enthusiasm for my appearance.

I did four shows a day and five on the weekends. During this stint I stayed at a hotel near Times Square. I could peek out the curtains and see my name on the marquee at the Roxy. One evening, looking through the twilight snowfall, I watched the marquee lights blinking on and off, my name spelled out in big letters topping the other attractions. Long lines of people were standing in the bad weather, waiting to buy tickets. My knees turned to jelly and my feet to stone as I thought, "Why's all this happening to me?" For one of the few times in my life, I was thoroughly scared. Fortunately this terrible case of stagefright didn't take place onstage.

Outwardly I always tried to maintain some professional calmness when performing. But that night when I went through the backstage door for my opening at the Roxy I was bubbling inside like a volcano. This internal "juice" is probably the source of an entertainer's energy. It's the part of his temperament that sends him out to face a horde of strangers and turn them into friends. When you sign that contract to perform, you promise to care more than the audience. Certainly you demand more from yourself than an audience ever could.

This photograph was taken outside the Warfield Theatre in San Francisco. It gives an idea of the lines that greeted me during my headlining run at the Roxy in New York.

My stage act was an encore-type performance. The way you move onto a stage, off it, and then return is clearly worked out long before showtime. My act would end; I'd go offstage, wait to be applauded back on, retire again, and then do another number or two. These "call-backs" were rehearsed, and the lighting cues were mapped out with the stage manager and crew. This way of performing brought me notice as a "showstopper," but a spotlight doesn't automatically follow you like a robot. A master plan was always on file with the lighting crew. This in no way diminished the magic for the audience. They liked the way I presented my act. I catered to my audience, neither overwhelming them nor ignoring them.

I had one standard rule for my act: come on singing. After a loud, bouncy opening number, I'd welcome the audience. Then I'd say, "Here's a song I wrote that helped me start eating regular." I'd play a familiar number. Next in the format came a suitable holiday song. The number-four spot was the time for "The Object of My Affection." That called for a stage bow afterward. When I was applauded back on, I'd express my appreciation and always salute the whistlers in the balcony.

The second section of my act relied on guitar playing, a novelty song, perhaps a dance step, and some other jokes. Finally I'd say, "Yes, folks, I really can sing," and then do a number that would let me use my full vocal range. After that a simple "Thank you very much" would be the conclusion. I'd return in the finale, in which all the acts were greeted, taking my final bows.

This format had been tested in most parts of the country, and I found that New Yorkers liked it too. The first weekend the Roxy took in $24,000. That's a lot when you consider it was all in twenty-five-cent and forty-cent tickets. The manager told me that it was approximately 25 percent higher than they'd expected. "We're doing our best business since Christmas," he said.

The trade paper *Variety* reviewed my act and decided that I was "lovable." I liked the line they used that said I succeeded in "ingratiating himself into the hearts of his audience."

After two weeks of steady success the Roxy management decided to hold me over. "Two more weeks," they agreed smiling. "That'll be the first time in history we've used a single headliner act for a full month."

I smiled but worried at the same time. "I don't know if I can keep pulling the crowds. This is February, and the weather's bad. Lent's coming. The subway strike is likely to louse things up for all of us." I was scared all over again.

On Sunday morning I walked around Times Square, wondering how a country kid just a couple of years out of college had managed to make theatrical history at the Roxy. *Variety* thought my success came from "working very naturally and not trying so hard." The paper was right about the natural part, but I was trying. Trying all the time, and trying damned hard.

I finished eighty-six consecutive performances at the Roxy in March. Later someone asked me about seeing the sights in New York. I answered honestly, "I didn't see a thing except my name up in lights."

17

Rita Hayworth

After New York I returned to the West Coast and work on a Twentieth Century Studio film entitled *Paddy O'Day*. This movie was part of Hollywood's love affair with all things Irish. *Peg O' My Heart* and *Smiling Irish Eyes* had already proved big hits. This movie was calculated to top the heap, using a new child star, Jane Withers.

The cast for *Paddy O'Day* included a girl who later became Hollywood's "technicolor love goddess"—Rita Hayworth. In 1936 she was still known as a Tijuana dancer by the name of Margarita Carmen Cansino. In typical Hollywood casting, Rita, who was American and passed herself off as Spanish, was signed to play the part of a Russian girl in an Irish film.

My part was as an ornithologist—a bird specialist. I was supposed to be a professor, and the makeup department told me to grow a mustache to look more "intellectual." I complied and, yes, that mustache was really pink.

Jane Withers's role was that of a brat. In real life she was cute, talented, and highly disciplined. She was about ten years old at the time, but had already graduated from kiddy acting school. She was a veteran of the Meglin Kiddies Studio, which taught juveniles the whole works—dancing, singing, poise, comedy, drama, and acting. On the set Jane obeyed the director and dialogue coach with total precision. She was easy to work with, a real pro despite her youth. By the way, the old theory is true: a kid or a dog in a film will always steal the scene.

Stage star Margaret Anglin once remarked that actresses didn't

I have my arm around Rita Cansino, later known as Rita Hayworth. This cast photo is for *Paddy O'Day* that featured Jane Darwell (*right*) as the governess and child star Jane Withers (*center*). My role was that of an ornithologist.

have husbands; instead, they had attendants. I might add that child stars didn't have agents—they had mothers. Jane Withers was no exception. "Star mamas" usually meant trouble on a set; the same thing could be said of the mothers of Shirley Temple, Sunny McKeen, Jackie Cooper, Freddie Bartholomew, and the en masse maternal power of the "Our Gang" mothers.

Jane Withers had made *Gentle Julia* at Fox in 1934 and *This Is the Life* in 1935. Later she played opposite Shirley Temple. Eventually she became perhaps even more famous in her television role as Josephine the plumber.

In a funny way Jane Withers wasn't the only child on the *Paddy O'Day* set. Rita Cansino and I were anything but old hands to some of Hollywood's intricacies. Rita had done a few bit parts in black-and-white movies such as *Under the Pampas Moon*. *Paddy O'Day* was her first film with a love scene.

The term "love scene," as done in 1936, deserves some explanation. It goes without saying that the love scenes were done fully clothed and in an upright position. The impetus for this unnatural position came from the Catholic Legion of Decency. This group had waged a long, hard campaign against "filth and violence" in movies. Even a hint of sex fell into their category of decadence. Most movies, despite their imagined immorality, remained sexless. Kisses were on the chin. The hero kept his arm around the girl's waist, and then for only twelve seconds. Bedroom scenes always showed twin beds, pajamas, dressing gowns, and full lights. The Catholic Legion actually thought it was better to imply separate bedrooms.

Paradoxically, movies were cleaner than ever at about the same time the behind-the-scenes casting couch was going strong. A lot of the Hollywood history that has come down to us was invented, but enough of it was true to provide scandal offscreen. Onscreen, however, the camera never showed any real sin. The story stressed that any high jinks were really only delicately sinful. The trick was for the leading man to ravish the heroine but always with good intentions leading to marriage. The fallen woman was always pure in heart, and all temptations were resolved into domesticity.

Screen kisses became a national preoccupation, with audiences tak-

A reigning screen star of 1936, Jane Withers was every bit a professional actress. She graduated from the Meglin Kiddies Studio and starred in *Paddy O'Day*.

ing note of first kisses as being as important as first kisses in real life. The screen kisses were always performed side to side; directors felt that nothing was communicated by seeing the back of one actor's head. Also, while a screen kiss might not lead automatically to pregnancy, it almost always led to matrimony. A whole generation of audiences was raised on the scorching fade-out kiss. As a lot of people have noticed, today's movies begin where yesterday's left off.

The dialogue surrounding the screen kisses was taken seriously by the audiences. It was a tightrope. The words had to be sentimental but believable. A peck on the cheek was sufficient to connote true affection. Looking soulfully into the eyes of the leading lady meant everlasting love. The America's sentimental vocabulary was enriched by such lines as "Here's looking at you, kid," "If you want anything, just whistle," and "Frankly, my dear, I don't give a damn."

Paddy O'Day didn't supply any memorable lines to our nation's cultural heritage, but it did offer the studio a chance to publicize Rita Cansino's first love scenes by inventing a romance between us. The idea of a lovely young starlet and a country boy from Oklahoma was a winning combination in the hands of an eager Twentieth Century Fox publicity man.

Rita and I were sent out on an arranged date. The plan was for us to visit the Cocoanut Grove at the Ambassador Hotel for dinner, then travel to various nightspots where we'd be seen and photographed.

On the appointed night the studio sent a long, black limousine to pick me up. The chauffeur then drove to Rita's family's house, and the date officially began.

Miss Cansino and I were not well acquainted. We tried to chat as we headed for supper. "Do you like the Ambassador?" I asked. "The Cocoanut Grove is one of my favorite spots."

"I don't know. I've never been there," she replied.

I should have caught on right then that Rita wasn't familiar with the nightspots and nightlife routine. She seemed poised, beautiful, and confident, however, and I gave her credit for being more sophisticated than she was. We ate dinner at the Cocoanut Grove, having a few cocktails before the meal, wine accompanying the steaks, and

Rita Hayworth and I exchange meaningful glances as part of a 1930's style "love scene." We also went out on a date arranged by the studio.

Brandy Alexanders afterward. Rita let me do the ordering. She didn't decline the drinks, so I had no way of knowing she was a nondrinker.

Another important matter that I didn't know about was her age. She had lovely dark hair, heavy makeup, sophisticated clothing, and a nice way of using her eyes that made me figure she was in her early twenties, perhaps twenty-four. I was twenty-eight, so I thought we made a nice young couple. Later I was shocked to find out I was playing older man to her tender seventeen years.

As we polished off the last of the brandy ices, Rita exclaimed, "It's been a lovely evening. It's too soon to go home."

"I quite agree," I responded, deciding that we'd take the limousine over to the Club Alabam, where my friend Louis Armstrong was holding forth. The Club Alabam was on Central Avenue, in the heart of Los Angeles's Harlem.

When we went inside, I told Rita how Louis Armstrong had given me one of my first musical jobs playing on the riverboat at St. Louis.

"That's nice," replied Rita, hiding a yawn. I couldn't believe that she was sleepy, but I was noo naïve to understand that the wine and after-dinner drinks were bothering her.

Inside the Club Alabam, Louis Armstrong looked up, spotted me, and greeted me with the line, "Pinky, you sure have growed a lot since you was in my riverboat band."

"But I haven't outgrowed my banjo," I responded, inviting him to sit down and have a drink with Rita and me.

He joined us, and he and I reminisced about the old days. Louis Armstrong was as personable as ever with his gravel-harmony voice and keyboard smile. He'd acquired a nickname like me—only his referred to his large mouth. "Satchelmouth" was finally shortened to "Satchmo." His whole face gestured when he spoke. The studio photographers busily snapped pictures of Rita, Louis, and me.

After a few more drinks I finally noticed that Rita was caving in. "I think we better go home," I suggested.

"It's definitely past my bedtime," she admitted. In the limousine Rita confessed that she was ill. She put her head on my shoulder and closed her eyes.

I was in a quandary, feeling responsible for a rather dismal ending to what the studio had billed as a "night of fulfillment." "I'll get you home as fast as possible," I vowed.

She clutched my hands, "Daddy will kill me."

An irate father—something I didn't need in my evening! I knew that Rita's dad was an adagio dancer. If I brought his daughter home in this condition, he might just use some of that fancy footwork on me. I tapped our chauffeur on the shoulder. "Find a phone booth and pull over."

My theory was: when in doubt, call home. An apartment on Hayworth Avenue was my current home. My roommate was college friend Duke Taylor. I knew Duke would have an idea about how to handle my situation.

He listened and then said, "Bring her over here. Taking her home to daddy would be cutting your own throat."

We went to the apartment, found a swimsuit for Rita, and encouraged her to take a late-night dip in the apartment's outdoor pool. Duke took lifeguard duty. I made a pot of strong coffee.

The swim and caffeine did the trick. When Rita was awake enough to say, "Take me home," I complied in a hurry. My courage faltered again when she fell asleep in the car. It was now nearly four in the morning. Fresh air, I thought desperately, telling the chauffeur to stop at the park. Rita and I took a long walk in the vicinity of the La Brea tar pits and then proceeded on down Wilshire Boulevard to the Miracle Mile area where she lived. As we pulled up to her house, the driver turned off the car lights and killed the motor, and we coasted to a stop.

I whispered, "Can you make it in all right?"

She nodded, took off her shoes, and tiptoed across the sidewalk in ladylike steps. She didn't need any help, and I was delighted with relief to see her safely inside the house.

We encountered no repercussions from our evening together. There was a weekend lapse in the filming, and when we met again on the set, Rita looked as beautiful and composed as ever. She took my arm, turned those gorgeous eyes toward me, and murmured, "Thanks—for everything." Her voice went lower. "You could have taken advantage of me."

"I'm about as old-fashioned as my image on those kinds of matters," I assured her. "I try not to let my enthusiasm outweigh my judgment."

She seemed to have confidence in my judgment after that. When we discovered that I was eleven years older than she, it seemed like a huge difference. She gave me credit for maturity as well as decency. One day she suggested that we go have some coffee together. "I want to talk to you about something personal."

When we were out of hearing range of curious coworkers, she confided, "There's a certain producer over at Fox studios. . . ."

She didn't have to tell me the man's name. He had a reputation throughout the industry. "He's made you the object of his propositions, right?"

"Yes, the usual line—if I'll be his casting-couch exclusive, he'll make me a big star." She bit her lip, obviously confused.

"Rita, don't fall for it," I advised. "You've got the charm and talent to make it big on your own merits. You're young—my God, yes, you're *young*. A lot younger than I thought you were that night we went on the date. With the kind of rare beauty you possess, you can afford to wait."

"What I am going to tell Mr. Bigwig?"

I told her what to tell him. We shared a good laugh, and then I talked to her about ways she might improve her career without falling prey to the casting-couch syndrome. "You might consider changing your name from Cansino. It types you as a Spanish dancer. You've got too much talent to be stuck in one niche."

Shortly after that Rita Cansino became Rita Hayworth. Her mother's name had been Volga Hayworth, and perhaps Rita remembered the evening she'd spent with me on Hayworth Avenue too. After the name change she went on to bigger and better parts, reigning as one of Hollywood's big names through the forties and fifties. She reigned in real life too, as wife of Ed Judson, Orson Welles, Aly Khan, Dick Haymes, and Jim Hill. At one point she had one of the richest and longest-running contracts in show business. Her great film successes, such as *Gilda* and *Sadie Thompson*, resulted in more pressure than she could handle either professionally or personally.

I congratulate Rita Hayworth after her acceptance of honors at the 1976 Thalian Ball.

Rita became another victim of the steam-cooker atmosphere around show-business personalities. It is exciting, it is heady, and it can be utterly consuming. Rita exhausted herself, spent a long time coming back, and now seems to be master of her own destiny once again. In November, 1977, the Thalians honored her for her contributions to the movie industry.

Debbie Reynolds, then president of the Thalians, sponsored the tribute with the theme, "You Were Never Lovelier." The Thalian Charity Ball is an annual affair. The twenty-second ball was held in 1977 at the Century Plaza Hotel. It was black-tie formal with cocktails, dinner, and show. The ballroom sold out to show-business people, businessmen, and fans, who thought Debbie Reynolds and producer Jimmie Baker did a marvelous job on the show. Proceeds from the benefit support the Cedar Sinai Hospital's community mental-health center.

At the Thalian Ball I was asked to do a small part in honoring Rita Hayworth. I told about filming *Paddy O'Day* and our first love scene together. It was wonderful to see Rita looking so lovely, and she seemed touched by the occasion.

Backstage after the ball I enjoyed renewing friendships with many show-business personalities. I saw Barry Sullivan, Glenn Ford, Gloria DeHaven, and Jane Withers. Ricardo Montalban came over to shake hands and complimented me by saying, "Pinky I still enjoy your songs. They're some of the cutest ones still around." Gene Kelly reminded me that he and his brother broke in their first dance act to "The Object of My Affection."

All in all I'd rate the 1977 Thalian Ball as a deluxe affair. Although I had been out of show business actively for twenty-five years, there remained a fraternal spirit that I found sincere and satisfying. Hollywood is sometimes prone to believe the worst gossip about its residents, but they're kind enough to believe the best about you too. Haven't you heard the saying, "Show business folks are always sincere—whether they mean it or not"?

18

"The Love Bug"

In 1937, Franklin D. Roosevelt was inaugurated for his second term as president. The first worldwide radio broadcast brought us the coronation of King George VI in London. San Francisco dedicated the new Golden Gate Bridge. Howard Hughes flew his airplane from Los Angeles to New York in a record seven hours and twenty-eight minutes. Joe Lewis knocked out Jim Braddock for the heavyweight boxing crown. Nylon was patented in 1937, but women ignored the "fake" silk stockings. People danced the big apple, attempted the jitterbug, and sang such songs as "Harbor Lights," "That Old Feeling," and "The Dipsy Doodle."

I wrote a song that year too. "The Love Bug Will Bite You If You Don't Watch Out" was the title. I realized that ten one-syllable words in the title might pose a problem, but I liked the alliteration of sounds and the easy, catchy rhythm. I set out to make the song a hit.

By 1937 I had some resources in the music world. I belonged to the American Society of Composers, Authors, and Publishers (ASCAP). This organization, active worldwide, monitors the use of its members' material and collects royalties for them. Joining ASCAP is not as simple as joining a trade union. A member must have credentials, recommendations, and a sponsor. Harry Tobias and Johnny Mercer had sponsored my entrance into ASCAP in 1935–36, making me one of its youngest members. Almost all songwriters today belong to ASCAP, BMI, or the European counterpart, SESAC. Copyright laws have become increasingly complex as juke boxes, radio time, live performances, records, and tapes have come into worldwide use. An artist collects a small amount of money any time his music is used, even if it is only background for another show. Many nonmusical films or television shows use taped music for mood. In the case of "Love Bug" I collected a few cents every time the song was used for any purpose. Darla Hood, a fellow Oklahoman, sang the song in one of the "Our Gang" comedies. She was about eight years old and gave the music a cute twist by winking and wiggling her body. That "Our Gang" segment was shown in movie theaters, later on television, then at retrospectives of comedy, and now in classrooms. Every time it's used and Darla does her thing, I collect a few more pennies.

Long before a composer can sit back and collect his royalty checks, he has to get out and hustle his songs. In 1937, I had a verbal agreement with George Joy, of the Santly-Joy Music Publishing Company, to give him first chance at any new songs I wrote.

When I finished editing and rehearsing "Love Bug," I called Joy. We made an appointment, and I sang the song for him in his California office.

When I finished, he frowned. "Say that title for me again." He leaned back in his chair until both his legs and two legs of the chair were off the floor.

I deadpanned the long title.

"Kinda wordy, don't you think? How would we be able to get all that on a sheet-music cover?"

"Don't worry about cover pages. How do you like the song?"

He let his chair down with a menacing thud. "I like it a little, but it's too risky to publish. It's strictly a novelty. I don't think it's got the punch to be a commercial success."

Now what? I was disappointed, of course, but I didn't intend to head home with my tail between my legs. Instead, I'd do some personal song plugging. I believed in the song, novelty or not. I felt that if people heard it they'd enjoy repeating the title. Then they'd probably hum the verse and sing the chorus. "Love Bug" was a change from the slow, syrupy melodies of 1937, such as "The Moon Got in My Eyes," "Where or When," and "Blue Hawaii."

I plunged in to learn the fine art of peddling songs. I hadn't had to do promotion in the past three years. Now I discovered that the first order of the music business was to have about a hundred copies of the song printed. These professional copies would be left at radio stations, with recording companies, and with any artist who acted halfway interested.

I contacted performers who might use "Love Bug" on their radio shows. One gracious lady who took me up on my offer of a free song was Gracie Allen. The comedy and music team of Burns and Allen was one of the husband-and-wife shows that had really clicked. They worked in both films and radio. One of their early movies, *International House*, with W. C. Fields, remains a classic in comedy. On radio George and Gracie would do comedy skits that always ended with George saying, "Do the song, Gracie!"

Gracie Allen sang "Love Bug" on coast-to-coast radio. I was delighted that she could see the potential in the song.

I also paid a call on Ray McKinley. Ray was drummer with the Jimmy Dorsey band. "Sure, I'll help you out," said Ray. "Dorsey's band is doing Bing Crosby's 'Kraft Music Hall' next week. We can do the song then. How's that?"

"That's fine." Fine was a major understatement.

I widened my scope of calls to include a night venture to Louis Prima's Famous Door Club. Louis had been appearing at this nightspot for a long run. The Famous Door was a relatively small club. Crowds had to jam close together to get a seat. When Louis looked over the copy of "Love Bug," he smiled. "Lots of show people come down here. The exposure won't hurt."

"Exactly what I have in mind."

"I ought to warn you, though. Things have been a little slow lately."

"Looks like a good crowd tonight. Maybe if you'd do 'Love Bug,' it'd put the bite back in business," I encouraged.

He shook his head. "I haven't had time to run through it. I don't know how you interpret it."

I took Louis by the arm and escorted him to the alley. "I have plenty of time to show you the song, and we'll *make* a place to practice."

In the dark alleyway I took about five minutes to show him various gimmicks and riffs he could use to put the song over. A riff is a musical phrase, usually four bars of melody. "In the Mood" uses a riff, as do "One o'Clock Jump" and "Love Bug." A riff is used as a special modulation, a transition, or a turnaround point.

When we went back inside, Louis took five copies of the music to the bandstand. I went around front and squeezed through the door of the club. I saw Louis huddling with his band members, apparently briefing them on the quick change in their repertoire. Then he stepped to the microphone and said, "Folks, there's a crazy varmint loose in this place tonight. It's a love bug, and if you're not careful . . . well. . . ." Then he launched himself into a socko rendition of the song.

The audience loved his performance. I called Louis later and told him again how much I appreciated him helping me hustle the song. He laughed, "Heck, that song lifted the club right out of a slow spot. After the 'Love Bug' bit the Famous Door, we were held over for another ten weeks."

One friend of mine in southern California was a fellow songwriter. Harry Tobias and I had collaborated on several songs. Our combination of talents was easy going and workable. Harry had written many big hits on his own, including "Sweet and Lovely," "No Regrets," and "Sail Along, Silv'ry Moon." When I attempted to promote "Love Bug," I naturally turned to Harry for advice.

I explained my situation to him. "I'm going to go to Kansas City, Chicago, and New York to drum up interest in the song. Do you think I could leave some copies with you here on the West Coast?"

"I have a better idea than that, Pinky. Bring your music, your guitar, and yourself over to my house."

"Why?" I questioned. "Shucks, Harry, I know *you* like the song. That's what friends are for."

"That's what *relatives* are for, too. Don't you know Eddie Cantor is my cousin? He and I have worked together on lots of projects. I wrote songs for his revues back on Broadway. We'll drive over and let him hear your song. That would do a lot more for you than leaving sheet music on my doorstep."

Harry and I went to Cantor's home. I rehearsed in the car, aware that this special audition might land my song on the "Texaco Star Theatre." Cantor's production was one of the top radio shows, and

136

he'd been successful in movies, too. He'd made *The Kid from Spain*, *Palmy Days*, and some of the original Goldwyn musicals, such as *Roman Scandals*.

Before coming west, Eddie Cantor had been a topnotch vaudeville attraction. He'd been among the first Broadway performers recruited to the new talking pictures. He and Fannie Brice, Lillian Roth, Ann Pennington, and Mary Eaton had made early sound films on Long Island at a tiny sound stage that resembled a cave more than a motion-picture studio.

I was excited as I performed for Cantor, holding my guitar in one hand and the music in the other. Exposure on his radio show would mean almost certain success for "Love Bug."

When I finished, he said, "Hey, I like the song—and I like the way *you* do it."

"I'm available," I indicated happily.

"All right. We'll use you on the show."

I didn't give up my proposed swing to the East Coast, feeling that the song would need everything Cantor or I could do in its behalf and then some. But I breathed a lot easier after my guest stint on "Texaco Star Theatre."

Eddie Cantor told me, "Go on your trip. When you get back, we'll give you another shot on the show."

Before I took off for New York, I thanked Harry Tobias once more. He wished me well on my trip, saying, "Go east, young man, go east."

I couldn't resist asking, "Harry, by the way, do you have any relatives on the East Coast?"

For several weeks I barnstormed my way across the continent, calling on recording studios, disc jockeys, and nightclub performers. I made up in energy what I lacked in special contacts. I knocked on any door that read *Music Publisher*.

When I arrived in New York, I had twenty copies of sheet music left from my original one hundred. I knew precisely where to head with those remaining copies. The Glen Gray Casa Loma Orchestra was playing at the Rainbow Room atop Rockefeller Center. Thank God for old-time friends! Grady Watts and Pee Wee Hunt were both with the Glen Gray organization. Grady and I went all the way back to Oklahoma University and Boomer Band days. Pee Wee did a lot of the novelty songs for the Casa Loma band.

I caught the first show at the Rainbow Room and went backstage at intermission. In the locker room I went through a chorus of hellos, a deluge of warm handshakes, and a couple of quick beers. Grady Watts asked me, "What brings you to town? Just passing through?"

That was as much of an opening as I needed to pull the music from my jacket pocket. "As a matter of fact, I happen to have brought a new song along."

Naturally there was a lot of good-natured teasing about my being an opportunist, but the fact is that most performers enjoy finding new melodies. They are eager to hear new material and will go out of their way to seek it. Part of the natural curiosity that goes with being a creative artist helps musicians spot new tunes quickly. They love to sit around after hours and improvise melodies.

The thirties were a time of great originality in American music, the height of the jazz and swing eras. It was during this time that Toscanini was given carte blanche with the newly created NBC Symphony. Gershwin's *Porgy and Bess* added native American melodies to light opera. Duke Ellington composed sophisticated and elaborate piano concertos, such as *Black and Tan Fantasy*. My novelty song, "Love Bug," was a little bit off the beaten track of pop music, which didn't hurt it a bit. As I passed out the music, I pointed out some of the gimmicks I'd used.

Grady Watts could see the gleam in my eye. "All right, why don't you run through it for us?"

For once I tried to beg off, not having my guitar or time to warm up, and then suddenly I spotted Lester Santly entering the room. My nerve came back immediately. Santly was the other half of the Santly-Joy Music company. Now I was in a position to get a second hearing from that firm. Georgie Joy hadn't fallen in love with the "Love Bug," but perhaps it would bite Lester Santly. I immediately reversed my objections to doing the song. "Heck, I'll be a good sport. Let me do a quick version for you guys."

I demonstrated "Love Bug," keeping one eye on vocalist Pee Wee

Hunt and the other eye on Santly. When I finished, the band gave me a nice round of applause. Santly put up his hand as if asking permission to speak. "Say, who's the publisher of your little ditty?"

"I hope you are, Mr. Santly."

Glen Gray, the orchestra leader, broke in. "No more of this backroom stuff. Let's take this song out front and see how an audience reacts." He passed out copies to key bandsmen. "Pinky, I'll call you out later, and you do a few of your past hits and then introduce the new song."

Pee Wee Hunt suggested, "And I'll get busy and work on it for our next radio show." He did vocals for the band's Camel Cigarette's radio show.

All this sounded wonderful to me. I'd read that radio sales had topped eight million that year. Mutual had become the third national network. During favorite shows, such as "Information, Please," "Amos 'n Andy," or "Amateur Hour," Americans crowded around their sets. I didn't see any way for "Love Bug" to miss after exposure on the "Texaco Star Theatre" and the "Camel Cigarette Show." I thanked both Pee Wee and Glen Gray for helping the song along.

Glen Gray insisted, "If it goes over tonight, *you'll* be responsible," reminding me to get ready to go onstage.

My appearance in the Rainbow Room that night was considerably more "off the cuff" than when Claude Kennedy and I had performed supposedly spontaneously at the Baker Hotel in Dallas. Yet part of being truly professional means being ready on a moment's notice. Another part is cool nerve. Surely, if I believed in "Love Bug" enough to spend my money traveling coast to coast, I also had the fortitude to step out in front of the Casa Loma Orchestra and sing the song.

My impromptu spot was well received. When I'd finished and taken my bow, I returned to the stage wings. Santly asked me, "What's your next stop with that song?"

"Horace Heidt's band is playing at the New York Biltmore. I have a friend who does vocals with that band. I thought I'd drop by."

"Mind if I tag along?"

"Let's go." I tried to sound casual, but inside I was ticking with happiness. Santly obviously intended to check out the response at the

Biltmore. This meant that he was at least halfway interested in publishing the song.

The Horace Heidt band also did a popular radio show, the "Pot of Gold." Larry Cotton, my friend from university days, did vocals, as well as serving as a talented arranger.

At the Biltmore the audience loved the bouncy, catchy tune and lyrics of "Love Bug." I was pleased to see the smile on Santly's face. I had one more musical rabbit in my bag of tricks. "Now let's go over to the Roosevelt Hotel. Maybe we can catch the late show."

"And see Guy Lombardo, too?"

I nodded. "His arranger is another friend of mine, an Oklahoman who———"

"You people are everywhere!" interrupted Santly, but he seemed agreeable to hitting the Roosevelt.

Guy Lombardo had the reigning sweet band of the thirties. It had been at the Roosevelt for several years, parlaying the "sweetest music this side of heaven" into one of the largest musical fortunes this side of heaven. The radio sponsor for the Sunday show was Bond Bread.

My reception at the Roosevelt followed the pattern set at the Rainbow Room and the Biltmore. I was invited onto the floor to do my song. The reaction was enthusiastic. After performing my spot, Lombardo talked to me a moment. "Come by on Sunday morning, and we'll use your song on the radio show. It's a contest setup on the air with audience participation."

"I have faith in audiences," I said. "I'll be here Sunday."

The broadcast the following weekend presented several songs to the studio audience and then asked them to vote for their favorite. "Love Bug" won the popularity contest. Santly was in the audience, clapping the hardest. I was backstage biting my fingernails. When Guy Lombardo declared "Love Bug" the winner, he added, "And folks I'm glad you picked this particular song. The man who wrote both the words and music is in the wings backstage." There was applause from the audience. Lombardo motioned me onstage. "Come out and take a bow, Pinky Tomlin."

When the air time was up, Lombardo asked me to come out again. I ended by doing a twenty-minute show, including most of my previous hits. Santly waited patiently till I was finished. He patted me on the back and said, "Let's meet bright and early Monday morning to talk about a contract."

"Monday, bright and early," I repeated, grinning.

"My office is in the Brill Building on Broadway."

"Brill Building, Broadway." I knew that all the famous music companies headquartered there. "That's precisely the invitation I've been looking for ever since I left California." I thought it only fair to warn Santly that his West Coast partner, George Joy, hadn't been as enthusiastic about the song. "You'd better invest in a long-distance call to Joy. It's going to take both of us to convince him about 'Love Bug.'"

"I'll take care of Joy. You take care of our appointment Monday."

The weather turned sunny and clear on Monday morning, as if the whole world intended to shine and smile on my song. In the Brill Building elevator I noticed a tall man with sheet music under his arm. When it became apparent that we were both getting off on the third floor and heading for Santly's office, we introduced ourselves.

"I'm Hal Kemp," he said, "lining up a recording session for next week."

"I'm here to launch a love bug."

He commented, "Sounds cute." Later, in Santly's office, Kemp asked to hear the song. "We might use it next week. I have a vocalist who can really do justice to novelty numbers. His name is Skinny Ennis."

Santly and I were agreeable to the proposal. Skinny Ennis did a charming vocal, and his recording of "Love Bug" became one of my favorites.

Santly smiled as he made up the sheet-music contract. "We've already had quite a few calls for 'Love Bug.' So many people have heard it on various radio shows that it's going to hit the music stores presold. As for records, Pinky, do you have a recording contract anywhere?"

"Brunswick."

"Let me call them and try to get your recording of the song to coincide with our sheet-music publication."

The arrangements were worked out. While I was in New York, I recorded "Love Bug" on one side and "Country Boy at Heart" on the flip side. The Joe Haymes Band was in rehearsal in the city, and they provided the musical backup.

When I left New York, I had a fat contract for the song. Santly was most generous, even reimbursing me in cash for the money I'd spent touring the country to plug the song. He then took out a full page ad in *Variety* extolling the virtues of the song and suggesting that the contract I'd received was "unheard of." The ad told the roundabout way Santly-Joy had acquired the musical rights and said, "This song-writer is a Jesse James with a melody instead of a gun."

I thought the *Variety* sob-story ad was pretty cute. Certainly I knew enough to follow the old advice about money—cry all the way to the bank.

By the time I returned to California, "Love Bug" was number nine on the hit parade. It went on to sell thousands of copies of sheet music and tens of thousands of records. I again appeared on Eddie Cantor's "Texaco Star Theatre" and sang the song. It was icing on the cake now. The Cantor writers expanded my spot a bit, adding a few lines of dialogue. My part was simply the slow-drawl, snappy-comeback humor that I did easily. When the response proved excellent, Cantor offered me a contract as a regular on the show.

The idea of "regulars" had begun on the Rudy Vallee radio show for Sealtest Dairies. John Barrymore had been a guest, gone over big, and become a weekly part of the format. The Cantor show already had some fine talent. Deanna Durbin, Bert Gordon alias the Mad Russian, Jack Renard's orchestra, and announcer Jimmy Wallington were all regulars.

The producer and director of the Cantor radio show was a talented twenty-four-year-old, Vic Knight. We became friends and later collaborated on such songs as "Old Fashioned Christmas." Vic was among the cleverest of the young writers associated with radio during this period and added a lot of show-business know-how to the Cantor vaudeville format.

I joined the "Texaco Star Theatre" cast. During this time I was also performing at the Orpheum Theatre in Los Angeles. Of course, I kept one eye on the Hit Parade charts, watching "Love Bug" climb all the way to number two. It stayed on the charts for several months. "Love Bug" was one of six songs I wrote that proved to be Hit Parade material.

"Love Bug's" story had a happy ending, but its beginning had been far from certain. I had been an audience of one who thought it had potential. This quality of being convinced of the worth of something creative is important to any artist. It would be lovely if there were crystal balls to show us the destiny of our creations. But stubborn, single-minded determination did as much for "Love Bug" as any magical combination of promotion or destiny.

I'd say matter-of-factly that, if you want to write songs as a hobby, it's fun, but if you want to do it as a business, it's tough. Taking "Love Bug" on the road was an act of faith. It was about in the same category as the time I'd hitchhiked from Durant to Norman because I wanted to go to college. Some of the good things that resulted from both trips can be attributed to luck. But as Branch Rickey once noted, "Luck is often merely the residue of design."

19

Mrs. Pinky Tomlin

A special happiness came my way in the fall of 1937, when Joanne Alcorn moved to California. She had been my friend ever since that night in 1933 when I'd first sung "The Object of My Affection" at her home in Ponca City, Oklahoma. We'd later seen each other at Oklahoma University, and, since moving to the West Coast, I'd written and called her occasionally. On several trips east, I'd even rented a car and gone to see her. She had a special place in my affections, but I'd never been brave enough to admit that to her.

When I left Oklahoma to seek my fortune, she had been seventeen. Now, at twenty, she was moving to Los Angeles to finish her education at UCLA. She called me, and we enjoyed reminiscing about college days. She asked, "Do you remember the time you were singing 'Object' at a prom and I danced by and winked at you?"

You bet I remembered. "That was the evening I told you, 'Go away, pretty brown-eyed baby and see me when you grow up.'"

She laughed, "Well, I'm taking you up on the offer to come back later."

I was more than eager to renew our friendship. Immediately I made a date with her. When we met, I saw that the last three years had been good to both of us. Joanne was simply gorgeous at twenty, with the kind of grown-up beauty I'd been waiting for. Now I could finally admit that she'd been the object of my affection all along.

Our engagement was announced in October, 1937. Eddie Cantor started a deluge of publicity by quipping, "Pinky, the Love Bug bit you and now you're marrying the object of your affection." Photographers and fan magazines had a field day with that line. Pictures of

Mrs. Pinky Tomlin, the former Joanne Alcorn of Ponca City, Oklahoma.

Joanne and me were plastered coast to coast and even as far away as Europe and South America.

A lot of fanfare surrounded us, but we were both basically private people. Before we were married, we made each other not only the usual promises but also an important one concerning show business. We decided that our private life had to be of paramount importance. If that meant fewer movies, promotional tours, theater bookings, or whatever, that's the way it would have to be.

We were married in Joanne's mother's home in Westwood Hills on March 22, 1938. After the ceremony, performed by Reverend Harold Proppe, we tried to take a short honeymoon in Santa Barbara. I say "tried," because my friends put a lot of obstacles in our way. We had put out a publicity release saying that we were going to Hawaii, hoping to discourage fans. Then we headed north on the freeway. My so-called friends had notified the California Highway Patrol and alerted the police to be on the lookout for our car. The cops pulled me over, insisting, "You're driving erratically. Get out and walk the white line."

After that encounter we checked into the Biltmore in Santa Barbara. Joanne discovered that her sister had tied all of her trousseau in knots. We were bombarded by telegrams and phone calls from the few people who knew where we were. When we finally took the phone off the hook and refused to answer the door, the bellhop took to pushing messages under the door. One of them was from my friend the writer Al Martin. It was addressed to Joanne and read, "Don't let that Oklahoma kid fool you—that ain't Hawaii."

Later in the fall we took an extended trip east, visiting friends in Oklahoma as well. After that we settled into a fairly secluded life. We were sociable in our own way, entertaining close friends for supper and attending sporting events.

Joanne and I shared an interest in horses. We enjoyed the races at Santa Anita, joined the Turf Club, and later owned horses of our own. Joanne had inherited this interest from her father, oilman John Alcorn, who had owned a string of polo ponies. She had watched her father play polo in the spring at Colorado Springs, Colorado. His friends had included Fox Studio head Darryl Zanuck, who later

Joanne entertains while I look bashful at one of our western-style home parties.

bought the string of ponies from Alcorn. Joanne was a horsewoman in her own right. She showed jumping horses in competition in Kansas City and Colorado Springs while she was growing up.

After our marriage we attended of necessity some of the Hollywood parties. I wouldn't rate the movie industry bashes as orgies, but some of them ranked as bacchanals. Joanne was impressed by how hard everyone worked at these soirées. Performers under contract were required to be present as guests of honor. Most were expected to have a skit or song ready to add to the festivities. Once Joanne asked me, "Is all this necessary? All this hobnobbing with producers and always asking about their future plans? It seems everyone is constantly on display."

"That's a big part of this business," I admitted, "and one I don't particularly like. Cocktail parties, per se, are rather passé in my opinion."

"I don't need this," she smiled, "and neither do you."

"Well spoken. Let's find our coats and get out of here."

We made a rather permanent exit from the filmland society scene. After that we usually entertained at home, sometimes using a western motif and featuring music by Roy Rogers and the Sons of the Pioneers. Later I wrote a song for the Oklahoma State Junior Chamber of Commerce that became a popular addition to our parties. The title was "In Ole Oklahoma." It was adopted as state song for a while in the late thirties, before the musical *Oklahoma!* appeared on Broadway. There was a certain amount of truth in the verse that went, "Where ever I may be, where ever I may roam, I always seem to see the place I call my home." Joanne and I both kept our ties to our home state strong.

Was our attitude provincial? Perhaps, but we were products of the great Midwest and couldn't change our small-town backgrounds. There were a lot of good things associated with such a country-boy heritage. I have to admit that marriage, settling down, and stepping away from the forced glamour of Hollywood suited me perfectly. Many times I repeated one of the lines that had been associated with my homespun act, "Yeah, I'm dist-a-doin'-fine."

20

Texaco Star Theatre

Most of my energy went into radio as the thirties drew to a close. Eddie Cantor was busy making a film at Twentieth Century Studios. Texaco asked me to be his summer replacement. It sounded like a lot of fun, especially when Eddie came back as a guest and I got to introduce *him* as one of *my* discoveries.

One evening I invited Eddie to go with me to the Hollywood Legion Stadium to see a boxing match. The Friday-night fights were not only sporting events but also spotlight events for local celebrities. Between each round in the matches the house lights would be turned up. Famous—and not so famous—people timed their grand entrances to catch the lights.

Shortly after Cantor and I were seated, we heard a chorus of "ooohs and aaahs" from the audience. Turning around, I saw my old friend Robert Taylor making his entrance, but the cheers and wolf whistles weren't for Bob. They were meant for his gorgeous platinum-blonde date, Jean Harlow. Bob and Jean made a dazzling couple. By coincidence they took the seats directly in front of Eddie and me.

The lights dimmed, the fight went on. At the next intermission, I leaned forward and tapped Bob on the shoulder.

We hadn't seen each other in about three years. After our trip to Durant to premiere *Times Square Lady*, he'd gone on to great fame and success. I chuckled, remembering his doleful remarks about wanting to trade bank accounts. Now that he was a matinee idol, it seemed like a good time to remind him of the offer.

We greeted each other like old buddies. Bob said, "Boy, I'm glad to see you! This is great!"

"Are you sure you're glad to see me?" I teased. "Actually I came by to collect from you. We're supposed to trade bank books. Remember?"

He hastily assured me, "No way! The deal is off!" Then he scratched his head, frowning. He saw that I was keeping company with Eddie Cantor and knew I'd been doing "Texaco Star Theatre." He laughed, "Well, I don't suppose you've been camping out the last couple of years, Pinky. Maybe we ought to consummate the bargain after all."

We shook hands and laughed, even though we never got around to trading checkbooks.

During the evening Eddie Cantor and I talked about the radio show. He told me, "My contract doesn't have too much longer to run. I'm thinking about moving to a variety show for Camel Cigarettes."

I remembered his remarks during the time I was his summer replacement. Certain changes seemed to be in the air. The Texaco public-relations chief, James Tinery, asked me if I'd be interested in taking over the show if Cantor left. There was no official contract talk, only casual questions and answers. However, word of our discussion must have leaked back to Cantor. Suddenly I found myself with less and less to do on the show. When the summer ended and Cantor took the show over again, my guest parts were written out entirely. My musical numbers were cut, and finally I was eliminated from the scripts. I had five weeks left on my contract, but it was useless even to show up for rehearsals with nothing to do. Cantor was cool toward me, and finally one of his aides told me the obvious, "Your services are no longer needed on this show."

I had a hard time for the rest of that year, because most other radio shows were already booked. I felt that a lot of misunderstanding had led to gossip that wasn't accurate. Hollywood is a great town for industry rumors. I later learned that the Cantor episode had me pegged as "hard to work with." I wrote letters both to Cantor and to his agent, Abe Lastfogel at the William Morris Agency, trying to clear up the situation. This was a sad episode in my career, resulting in damage that put me back several rungs on the ladder of success. The only thing I knew for certain was that I couldn't stand around waiting for people to unlock their doors and welcome me back inside. I'd have to go out and knock again. A famous Hollywood writer once said of this kind of situation, "You have to say, OK, you can break my contract—but you can't break my heart."

In slapstick comedy, if you take a fall, you never land on your feet, but I made up my mind to come up on both feet. I felt I was a born survivor. When all else went haywire, I always had my music to fall back on.

21

On the Road

When I call music my "love," I mean exactly that. H. A. Overstreet provided many musical artists with a clue to their own psychological makeup when he wrote, "Sorrow, gladness, yearning, hope, love, belong to all of us, in all times and in all places. Music is the only means whereby we feel these emotions in their universality."

In 1938, I turned to my first love, music, to put my career back on its feet. When I learned that the Biltmore would have an opening for a big band in the fall, I approached them with the idea of forming the Pinky Tomlin Orchestra. The idea of going back to the Biltmore Bowl with my own band thrilled me. I had a special spot in my heart for the place that had been the scene of my first professional breakthrough.

Conditions for making music at the Biltmore were marvelous. Acoustics, appointments, and physical layout were splendid—it was the best place I ever played. The house policy of no cover charge and no minimum meant a full house every night. I thought that having an orchestra at the Bowl would be close to heaven. I had another good reason for not wanting to be on the road doing personal appearances. Our daughter, Sylvia, was born in December, 1938.

One of the first people I called to tell the good news was our family friend Josephine Dillon. She came right over to the hospital to keep me company while waiting for Sylvia's appearance in the world. Josephine and I had been close ever since she'd coached me at her speech school. It was while we were sharing the hospital vigil of waiting that the big news of the Gable-Lombard romance broke. Because

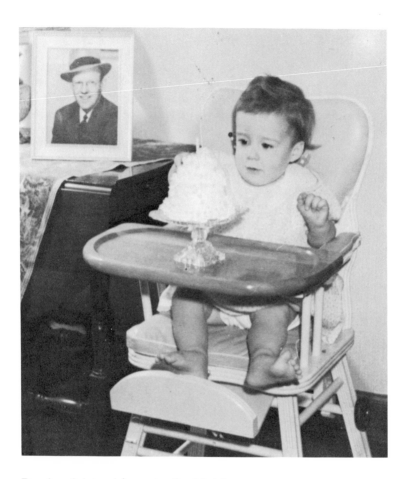

Daughter Sylvia celebrates her first birthday.

Josephine had been Gable's first wife, the press tracked her to the waiting room and deluged her with calls. What did she think of Clark and Carol running off together? She took the phone and squelched the interview by saying, "Carol and Clark? Oh, for heavens sakes, I couldn't care less! Don't bother me—I'm having a baby!"

Josephine Dillon was a woman of great dignity. I've always appreciated what she did for me both professionally and personally.

A new daughter at home was an added incentive to get my band going. The Pinky Tomlin Orchestra formally opened at the Biltmore Bowl in March, 1939.

There is quite a trick to sounding like a "big" band. Even with good acoustics, your volume has to be carefully controlled. Waiters will complain if you play too loudly; customers will complain if you play so softly they can't dance.

Commercial band music is meant to be easily digested along with dinner. It's fairly simple, because the out-of-town businessman wants to be able to dance the steps he learned twenty years ago. Big bands that played the major hotels have to have a potpourri repertoire. We'd do waltzes, ballads, watered-down jazz, show tunes, a polka now and then, perhaps a Latin-American number, and a holiday song if appropriate. There was never a night we weren't asked to do the "Anniversary Waltz."

The big-band sound was quite popular despite the continuing poor economic conditions of the land. Grim war news from Europe and soaring grocery prices at home kept people concerned. Porterhouse steak was up to forty-five cents a pound. Hamburger was selling for an unheard-of nineteen cents a pound. John D. Rockefeller died with a net worth of one billion dollars, but unemployed men still lined street corners selling nickel apples.

Despite the conflicts in the country, people still flocked to hear the big bands. Benny Goodman had ushered out jazz and ushered in swing music at a Palomar concert in 1935, and the nation had never been quite the same. Goodman now reigned as the king of swing, and a whole generation of bobbysoxers had invented a new vocabulary, including "dig it," "hep cat," "jive man," "out of sight," and "cool."

The dances young people favored were equally colorful, including the big apple, the lindy hop, the shag, and the jitterbug.

A big band implied a large number of instruments and musicians. A swing band might have four saxophones, seven brass, three trumpets, and four trombones. Most groups used arrangements in four-part harmony that gave a smooth, sweet sound. Each band tried for a distinctive "voicing." This means arranging music to convey a particular sound that becomes that band's trademark. The most easily recognizable voicing was done by Glenn Miller's band, which used the clarinet playing the lead melody in harmony with the sax section.

Most swing bands featured their drummers. Gene Krupa and Buddy Rich were especially popular. Sometimes the bandleader did featured numbers, such as Dorsey on trombone and Goodman on clarinet. Red Nichols and his Five Pennies were always a good drawing card, and many cornet players tried to imitate Bix Beiderbecke.

Big bands were a staple of radio in the late thirties. The National Biscuit Company sponsored "Let's Dance" every Saturday night from eleven until two in the morning. Fifty-three stations carried the program in its entirety. Nearly everyone in the nation could identify "I'm Getting Sentimental over You" as Tommy Dorsey's theme song and "Let's Dance" as Goodman's.

Big bands meant big money too. Paul Whiteman and his organization had proved that back in the 1920s, grossing over one million dollars a year with twenty-eight bands playing under his name. An early talkie movie, *The King of Jazz*, had featured Paul ("Pops") Whiteman. His band had served as training ground for both Dorseys, Eddie Lang, Joe Venuti, Al Rinker, Harry Barris, and Bing Crosby and the Rhythm Boys.

There were approximately thirty big-time dance bands at the beginning of the 1940s. Fewer than half survived the war years. During that time many bands went to a "sweet" sound that added more violins. Freddie Martin and Guy Lombardo used the sweet sound, tailoring it to the hotel or country-club trade. Freddie Martin once said, "I'll never stand in front of a bad band." To my knowledge, he never did.

155

At the Biltmore Bowl, the Pinky Tomlin Orchestra tried for a mix of sophistication, easy listening, and excitement. Opening night was more like a homecoming than a tryout for me. The band settled in and then played straight through from March until September, 1939.

During this period my friend Johnny Hyde approached me with an agreement to use the William Morris Agency as my representative. I had mixed feelings. There was no doubting the power of the huge Morris Agency, but my dealings with them in the Cantor matter had not been reassuring. Johnny Hyde convinced me that I should sign when he said, "Part of having a big band is the inevitable nation-wide tour. It would be to your advantage to have someone to do the booking." I signed with Morris, but since I had secured the Biltmore booking on my own, they received no commission from that engagement.

Soon it became obvious the agency wanted me to get started on the coast-to-coast tour. They scheduled my band for some local spots, then a few close-by dates, taking a hefty 20 percent of the contract price on all one-nighters. The agency policy was the hiring party had to send 50 percent of the total fee at the time of signing the contract. This meant, in essence, that the William Morris Agency held half of my band's money in advance. Sometimes it was quite a long time before we actually played the date. The agency might have twenty or thirty future appearances in the book for us. Ed Fishman of the agency once told me, "We'll book any date, anywhere, then worry about how to fill it." Unfortunately for the bands involved, the distances between engagements could be long and the time short.

It's my suspicion that booking agents knew the geographic location of New York, Chicago, and Los Angeles but that everything in between was unknown territory. Sometimes we were set up for an overnight stint in Dallas, followed the next night by Kansas City—a seventeen-hour drive in those days. Some bookers tried to keep dates along the route of the New York Central or the Santa Fe railroad. Most simply accepted a date on your behalf and then let you worry how to get there.

In September, 1939, the Pinky Tomlin Orchestra set out to tour the nation. I reviewed the schedule and threw up my hands in dismay.

"Look at this!" I wailed. "We're supposed to go from Los Angeles to Phoenix, El Paso, Albuquerque, Dallas, and El Dorado, Arkansas— all in ten days." The only comfort I got from the agency was the grudging admission, "Yeah, it's a pretty tight schedule."

During the next year we visited over thirty states, doing mostly one-nighters. Some notable exceptions were the four weeks we stayed at the Jung Hotel in New Orleans, the month at the Sylvan Beach in Houston, the six weeks at the Drake in Chicago, and the two months at the State Line Country Club at Lake Tahoe. The stint at Tahoe was the most beautiful spot on our agenda, but we were too tired to appreciate it by then.

Touring America with a dance band is a unique way to see and understand our country. I don't recommend it. If politicans were required to travel this way, they'd certainly come to understand our people's likes and needs a lot better.

No one has ever written a kind word about a musician's life on the road. There are rewards, but you're too tired to notice them. Louis Armstrong summed it up for every bandsman who has experienced the grind of one-night engagements. He said, "I feel like I spent nine thousand hours on buses, planes, getting there just in time to play with cold chops, come off too tired to lift an eyelash."

The irony of crisscrossing the nation was that folks really wanted to hear you in person. People had an urge to see for themselves the bandsmen they'd heard on the radio. Places like the Palladium in Los Angeles and the Aragon and Trianon ballrooms in Chicago were full every single night. Fans came up to the bandleaders and shook hands, perhaps trying to discover how the maestros produced the music. Wayne King, Eddie Duchin, Ted Weems, Art Kastle, and Fletcher Henderson were all playing the tour circuit about this time, and all were playing to packed houses. The record of Benny Goodman's 1938 Carnegie Hall Concert continues to sell forty years later.

Behind the scenes of big crowds and happy fans lay a lot of miles on a chuggy bus. The Pinky Tomlin Orchestra traveled on a chartered bus with a professional driver. There were sixteen band members, an instrument manager, and a road manager. A road manager's troubles make the biblical Job's look simple. A band manager has to deal with hotel reservations, bookkeeping, payroll, local unions, and the American Federation of Musicians. James Caesar Petrillo, who headed the AFM, displayed an irritating lack of common sense in calling wildcat musicians' strikes. Most band members were young, hungry, and eager to perform. The union brought them as much hassle as help.

During the year's travels we played nearly two hundred different engagements. Our resident female vocalist was Jeanne Darrell, who traveled on the bus with us, along with her chaperone, her mother.

Sometimes our paths crossed those of other bands. In Mitchell, South Dakota, we played the Corn Palace the night after Lawrence Welk. He stayed over and saw our show, and then we all went out for refreshments—meaning beer for most of us and milk for Welk.

My wife, Joanne, was traveling with me at this time. She and Lawrence Welk hit it off immediately. He confided to her, "I'm thinking of making this 'champagne music' my trademark. What do you think?"

She told him, "I don't think it'll go over very well. I'm afraid you're on the wrong track."

That was one of the few times her musical judgment was wrong. Once we heard a new singer, Frankie Laine, at a small nightclub. She immediately predicted great success for him. I doubted it, commenting, "No, I don't think he'll make it in this trade."

Joanne always claimed she wasn't musical, but she had a talent for making good snap judgments on new material. She could usually pick a hit after listening to it only once. I'd ask her how she could be so certain when she'd barely heard the lyrics and melody through. She'd only smile and shrug. I never did find out her knack, but she was right most of the time. It was downright discouraging to a professional musician. I admit that I had a tough time calculating a song's chances even with my college training, professional credits, and study of current markets. When I'd try out a new song on Joanne, she was honest enough to tell me if she didn't like it. She was often right as rain.

The tour was hard work for all of us. In thirteen months and forty thousand miles we missed only one engagement. When we were in El Paso, Texas, in the middle of winter, we discovered that our itinerary called for us to be in Albuquerque, New Mexico, the next night and then back in El Paso the following evening. Claude Kennedy, my longtime friend, who was now with the band, looked at the map and exclaimed, "That's a thousand miles from here."

Actually the distance was only a little over two hundred miles, but the terrain included some of the nation's roughest. I glanced at the threatening storm clouds and wondered how we were going to negotiate bad roads and make it to Albuquerque and back in twenty-four hours. "How's the wather?" I asked cheerlessly.

Claude snorted, "The weather? In winter? Do you have to ask?"

Our one choice was to take off into the night. Eventually the music union put a limit on the distance between one-night bookings, but in 1939 we didn't yet have the benefit of that rule. We pulled on overcoats and hustled our instruments onto the bus as a few snowflakes dusted the windows. "We'll be lucky to meet ourselves coming and going," I told the driver.

"I know a shortcut," he volunteered. "It'd save us at least fifty miles—cut an hour and half off the trip."

"Let's try it," I agreed, aware that time and distance were important. We also paid for the bus at the rate of forty cents a mile. A fifty-mile shortcut would save us twenty bucks. An extra hour and an extra dollar were both important to the band's success. "You're the boss," I told the driver. "Let's roll."

Our bus was equipped with the latest-model air conditioning—windows that leaked the winter air. The heater was usually broken, and the defroster was temperamental. Our only protections against the New Mexico blizzard were overcoats and Thermos jugs of coffee. Soon after we crossed the state line heading north, the snow came down in earnest. The paved highway turned into a gravel road, and then the gravel gave way to mud and slush. Claude Kennedy looked out the window and began a lonesome rendition of "Bury Me Not on the Lone Prairie." Ahead I could make out the shapes of snow-covered mountains. Perhaps we should change our theme song to "No Place like Home."

We settled down, and most of the band tried to sleep. Snow blotted out the scenery, such as it was. The road was nothing but bumps and mire. The driver plowed ahead bravely. I tried to doze, dreaming of warm southern California.

Suddenly we were snapped awake by a terrific jolt. The bus jerked in the middle and then stopped. There was no explosion or noise, only the abrupt halt and total silence. Sleepily I called, "What's happened?"

The driver's voice sounded meek. "This blasted shortcut seems to have turned into a dead end."

Claude Kennedy sat up, rubbed his eyes, and stared at the mountain ahead of us. He looked at the three feet of snow piled over the bus bumper. "Hey," he asked, "just how far *are* we from *where* are we?"

Our location turned out to be ten miles from Vaughn, New Mexico. None of us knew that at the time; all we knew was that we were stranded for the night. Occasionally, behind us, we heard thuds as other hardy travelers discovered the end of the trail. By morning, when we could see out through the snow, there were two trucks, our bus, and four cars stacked up in the drifts.

Our sax player said, "Wonder what our families think with us incommunicado."

"Ha! Wonder what our booking agent thinks," I replied. I knew that our contact in Albuquerque would be anxious and angry by now.

About midmorning the National Guard and a snowplow arrived to liberate us. A cheer went up from the stranded motorists. By the time we were extracted from the drifts and escorted into Vaughn, it was apparent that we couldn't get to Albuquerque in time to keep our date. When we called and related our troubles, the Albuquerque people were reasonably understanding. What else could they be? "Now," I told the bus driver, "take us back to El Paso, and no shortcuts."

Later I totaled up that the twenty-dollar saving on the proposed shortcut had cost me a play date in Albuquerque at eleven hundred dollars. We'd made a lot of long-distance phone calls assuring our families that we were all right, too. Add in the food at Vaughn, and I figured that the excursion into the New Mexico countryside had cost us a week's profit. On the other hand, we certainly didn't have a hotel bill for that night.

In El Paso again, we joined up to play a three-night job with the

Earl Carrol Vanities. I also sent a special delivery packet to William Morris in Los Angeles. It contained a topographic map of Texas and New Mexico. In red ink I drew the route of our travels, trying to impress them how ridiculous our bookings had been.

When the musician's union finally established rules about distances, we were all glad. That booking rule is about the only good the union ever did us. Our band manager spent a lot of time just keeping peace with the locals. Every place we played we had to pay a tax or make a contribution to the local union fund. Each town set its own scale. The local heads were often barbers, shoe salesmen, or plumbers who knew nothing about music. They sure knew about unionism, however. Usually they were out front waiting for us when we drove up to the hall. Often the local officials would insist that we pay the tax even before we set up our instruments. Our band manager would complain: "We're good for it. Give us a chance to get squared away."

"No, pay now. We have other spots to cover." This "several-spots" excuse was common. Then the union guys would collect our contribution, sit back, and watch our show. We came to the point of dreading to deal with the unions. They were one of the complex and unrewarding parts of the tour.

It was hard to keep up the pace for a year. The normal routine was to play a job, leave immediately afterward, sleep on the bus, travel fast and hard, arrive at the next town with barely time to check into a modest hotel, freshen up, put on our tuxedos, set up the band, and perform again. Laundry was impossible, good food improbable, sleep abnormal, and accommodations poor. The "normal" tour life meant bus trouble, cancellations, and lost bookings.

Our road manager served as advance man, scouting ahead for decent accommodations. When we arrived in a town, the hotel would sometimes conveniently "forget" our reservations if something better had turned up. We were stood up by the hotel in Longview, Texas, because of an influx of local football fans for a high school game. Other times we hit conflicts with Shriners' or Elks' conventions. Anytime we hit town at the same time as these free-spending gentlemen, we could almost count on having to bunk at the YMCA. One night we arrived in a small Kansas community to find that our rooms had been

161

turned over to the Elks. "They can't do this!" I fumed. "That's the group that hired us!"

Protesting got us nothing. We freshened up in the school locker room. On another occasion we ended up sleeping in the local fire station. The worst situation was when we arrived in the middle of the South Dakota Badlands only to be informed that our accommodations had been taken over by hunters awaiting the opening of pheasant season.

Despite the travel and hotel conditions, very few band members dropped out during the tour. We had good musicians who wanted to play. The few vacancies that occurred were filled without trouble.

About the only catastrophe worse than a lost hotel reservation was a canceled performance. In the trade, when a group is canceled, they say they are "living on panic." A band on panic usually ends up broke and stranded. In the musical world the law of mix-ups states that if a cancellation occurs it will happen in midwinter a thousand miles from nowhere.

There were a few times when I ran short of funds to pay the band. Usually it was the fault of our booking agency, which took half the fee when the date was arranged and then sometimes forgot to send back our portion when the engagement was kept. I had several real donnybrooks with the William Morris Agency about this, continually requesting they send ahead the payroll. Of course it was a band expense to pay the forty-cent-a-mile bus charge plus anything connected with gasoline and repairs. Band personnel and equipment were our responsibility too.

All in all, I'd say that playing one-night stands is hell. Tommy Dorsey told the story of playing a theater where a smart-aleck kid threw a penny onstage. Dorsey looked at the coin and then remarked, "There's only one kind of animal that throws a cent." A coast-to-coast tour is rewarding for the applause from the fans, but the behind-the-scenes business end really smells.

22

Bull Durham in Chicago

Every performer hates a cold audience. The facilities at the Drake Hotel in Chicago in January, 1940, ensured a frozen audience. The Drake Hotel, on Chicago's swanky northside, suffered frigidity in its attitude and in its location by Lake Michigan. The main dinner-and-dancing room was the Gold Coast Room. My band checked in to pay the room during one of the coldest winters in Illinois history. The temperature outside was in the low twenties with a wind chill off the lake that felt like forty below.

The temperature inside the Gold Coast Room seemed equally cold. The bandstand backed up to huge windows overlooking the lake. Drake management insisted that the drapes be kept wide open so the diners could have a view. Another concern of the Drake officials was dress. They wrote into my contract that I was required to perform in white tie and tails. I had never worn the outfit; it didn't jibe with my image or the rapport I wanted with an audience.

I took my dispute to my agent. For once, the William Morris Agency backed me. Tommy Smythe, the Chicago representative, tried to convince the Gold Coast manager that my orchestra should use its casual approach, thereby adding warmth and bounce to a staid place. He explained, "Tomlin's band projects its image as old-fashioned and friendly. Stuff them in white tie and tails, and they'll look like freaks."

The Drake manager remained adamant. I rushed down Michigan Avenue in search of a shop that rented white ties and tails. Three hours before the opening I was still fuming as I stood fidgeting while the tailor fitted my new wardrobe.

When I returned to the hotel, Tommy Smythe phoned me again. "Got the monkey suit?"

I admitted grudgingly that I did.

Tommy was a born warrior who seldom admitted defeat. "One silver lining, I suppose. You'll look gorgeous for all the big names we're sending over to watch the show."

"Tell them to wear overcoats in that igloo. The temperature on that bandstand can't be above thirty. At rehearsal this afternoon, our trumpet player's fingers were numb."

He agreed, "You'll have to thaw this audience. Here's your guest list: Mary Martin, Sophie Tucker, Tony Martin, Ethel Merman, Ben Blue, and Betty Grable."

I was pleased that so many celebrities were in town but still concerned about my attire. "If they report that I look uncomfortable, they'll be darned right. Heck, in that suit I look like a penguin—which is appropriate for the atmosphere."

When I hung up, the bell captain came in and asked if there was anything I needed. "I need a fire to warm up tonight's guests," I grumbled.

Suddenly I had an inspiration. It was simply a gag unconnected with anything I was aware of. "Wait a second," I told the bell captain. "Could you get me some little sacks of Bull Durham tobacco? The small bags with the drawstrings and the cigarette papers attached."

He looked confused. "Yes, sir. You want a smoke?"

"Not me," I grinned, as I told him I wanted enough tobacco pouches to place on every ringside table of the Gold Coast Room. "Hop to it. When I go out there tonight, I want to see sacks everywhere—and I'll be wearing one in the handkerchief pocket of my white tie and tails, making sure the little Bull Durham tag is hanging out."

The bell captain laughed, assuring me that he was the man for the job. "I'll help you unsophisticate that room," he said, "but I won't let the manager see your new decorations—or we'll both be out of a job."

The night was New Year's Eve. When I stepped on stage to start the first show, I could hear the buzzing among the customers before the band started playing. I carefully adjusted my tails, raised my baton,

164

and signaled the band to get ready. The moment of truth was at hand for the Gold Coast Room.

We played a couple of numbers. The reception was polite, typical of a conservative Chicago audience. They were cool—but not any cooler than my band. We played several fast numbers to keep our circulation going, and then I went to the microphone to welcome the audience. "Ladies and gentlemen, I'm delighted that you're here to-night in the Cold Ghost—I mean, Gold Coast Room." The line drew chuckles and then applause.

The manager of the room, his wife, and Tommy Smythe were seated at one of the ringside tables. I glanced in that direction and saw that Tommy had shifted his gaze to the tablecloth. He frowned, put his hand up to shade his eyes, and gave me an "Oh, brother, what next?" look.

I pitched my remarks to the audience. "Have you found your favors on the tables? Thought we might use those sacks to help light a fire in this place. Now, if you're not familiar with the fine art of rolling your own, I'll be around at intermission to demonstrate how it's done." There was a nice round of clapping for the suggestion. I finished my welcome by saying, "Folks, tonight is not just the opening of the Pinky Tomlin Orchestra—it's the invasion of Bull Durham."

I had clearly taken the bull by the horns. Then I proceeded to stroll around the ringside tables, chatting with celebrities, showing them how to lick and stick a homemade cigarette. I saw the manager get up and deliberately stalk toward the exit. By the time I made it to Tommy Smythe's table he was holding his head. He whispered, "Pinky, I'm going to the nearest bar and get bombed. Don't look for me until after you've been fired."

Personally I was having a marvelous time, and soon the excitement became contagious. By intermission everyone was having a great time trying to produce a smokable product from the pouches and papers. Newspaper photographers were snapping pictures right and left.

The next morning every Chicago paper had feature pictures taken at the Gold Coast Room. One showed me grinning and holding up a tobacco sack like a rube while standing stiffly in my white tie and tails. There were lots of photos of celebrities trying to roll cigarettes.

Each little write-up mentioned my orchestra and where we were appearing. I couldn't have had better publicity if I'd spent a million dollars.

At midmorning I received a crisp, curt call. "See the manager in his office without delay." As I rode down in the elevator, I wondered whether the man had a sense of humor or whether I'd better start packing. I figured that even if I got fired, it would be a blessing. Anywhere was warmer than Chicago in January.

I walked into the manager's office. He went straight to the point. "Tomlin, I called you here to fire you."

I commented, "OK."

"But the maître d' called and said the Gold Coast Room is sold out for tonight."

"Well, that's OK too."

Suddenly he beamed me a smile that was full of sunshine and warmth. "I have to confess, I have never seen anything like you, Pinky. I thought when you started that backwoods act last night we'd be laughed out of hearth and hotel."

"You shouldn't have left so early. If you'd stuck around, you'd *really* have been horrified. People were actually having a good time in that place."

He admitted, "I was so angry last night that I called around town, trying to hire another bandleader to replace you in front of your own orchestra."

"Wrong. If I go, they go."

All this was beside the point. The man was smiling and shaking my hand the whole time. "Actually, I'm calling your agent right now. I want your date extended at least another two weeks."

I shuddered. Another six weeks in Chicago's frozen atmosphere!

I wish I could report that our stay at the Drake turned sunny and clear. Problems persisted. A big band encounters big headaches with unions, travel arrangements, tax consultants, and booking managers. My wife, after a month of being stuck in the Drake, complained that she felt worse than a kept woman. She took to walking along the lake, insisting that the fresh air was welcome even if it led to frostbite.

She didn't freeze, but she did end up with strep throat. I caught an ear infection. We both wound up in the hospital for a ten-day "vacation." While we were recuperating, we talked candidly about cutting short the tour. "You can't forfeit the dates that are booked," said Joanne, "but if I ever see California again, I'm not leaving."

"Me, too. This see-the-USA-in-a-bus is no life for us. We've given up privacy. We've given up our health. We've all but given up our dignity. When we get back to Los Angeles, we'll find some other way to make a living."

I started planning right then to disband the orchestra when we finished the tour. We played out our contract, spending our last engagement at the beautiful State Line Country Club on the California-Nevada border. After that, Joanne and I said our good-byes to the band and drove straight through to our home in Los Angeles.

When we pulled in the driveway, we both cheered, and then we didn't bother to go inside the house. Instead, we went around and opened the trunk of the car. Inside were the stacks of musical arrangements that had been our life for the past year. Working quickly, we carried the huge musical library to the incinerator. We left about thirty thousand dollars worth of arrangements piled in the trash container. I stepped back, lit a match, and let the whole thing go up in smoke.

As we watched the blaze, Joanne remarked, "Wish we'd had some of that heat in Chicago."

"This is really quitting the band business in a flaming exit."

We went in the house, ready to start a new life. I was relieved to be done with the tour and the orchestra. The physical toll of living on the road for a year had been tremendous. Never in my life had I felt so wrung out.

It didn't worry me too much that I was uncertain what I'd do next. I'd never been afraid to burn bridges—or sheet music—behind me. I'd left Durant with nothing much but a guitar. I'd come to California with little more than one song. I'd find something to do now. Anything would be a step up from coast-to-coast one-night stands.

23

Pinky Tomlin Oil Properties

Until Pearl Harbor made the film industry alter course, the chief product of the studios continued to be flimflam. George Jean Nathan said it best: "Hollywood impresses me as being ten million dollars worth of intricate and highly ingenious machinery functioning elaborately to put skin on baloney."

In 1938 and 1939 I made a series of short films that fell into the category of baloney. These movies featured Milburn Stone, Bill Elliott, Maxine Doyle, Toby Wing, and Carl Bailey. A couple were simply short subjects featuring my band or music. Universal put one out under the title *The Pinky Tomlin Band*. Another was done for Paramount at their Astoria Studio on Long Island, New York, and then finished in Houston. Its title was *The Music America Loves*. *Tickled Pinky* was a Universal short that featured me and Martha Tilton but no band of my own.

The 1938 picture *Down in Arkansas* was filmed for Republic Studios on location at Lake Arrowhead, California. Overalls and straw hat were my whole wardrobe. The movie depicted life in rural America as wholesome and downright nourishing to the soul. In real life, by 1939 a farmer had his hands full and his belly close to empty. The sheriff in films always chased the bad guys. In real life he more often had a foreclosure notice than a pistol in his hands.

Hollywood scriptwriters took the view that life on the land was grand—the same moving spirit behind the Broadway success *Oklahoma!* Talk about agrarian wishful thinking. Until war broke out in December, 1941, the Depression was still clinging to the land. Life on

Tickled Pinky was one of the short subjects done by Universal Studios. Martha Tilton was a villager, and I was the musical postmaster of a small town.

Martha Tilton was featured vocalist with the Benny Goodman orchestra and made the famous recording "And the Angels Sing." This scene is from the short subject *Tickled Pinky* made in 1939.

the farm was still a hard struggle—as it had always been. Young people headed for the cities the minute they were old enough. And what did they do when they got to town? Why, they went to the movies and saw films that showed rural life as one continuous hay-and-cornball. Hollywood was busy eulogizing an era that had died at least a decade before.

Everyone took the attitude that I was a "natural" for country-boy roles. I could do the kind of gag comedy that was featured in *Down in Arkansas* and do character comedy such as the professor role in *Paddy O'Day*. Reviewers commented on my "naïve and natural" style. My response would be that natural is a style but is never unprepared or unrehearsed. It is far, far from naïve.

The moviemakers went on producing fantasies while Americans were learning new words like *Blitzkrieg*, hearing of Igor Sikorsky's first helicopter flight, and preparing for selective-service registration. Roosevelt was reelected once again, this time on a platform of war intervention. Great Britain rushed to rescue her forces from Dunkirk's shores. The United States Navy began building patrol bombers. In 1940–41 the handwriting of war was on every wall except the high fences that surrounded the film-studio lots.

When World War II arrived, it shook the motion-picture industry back to reality overnight. Pop songs on the hit parade such as "You Are My Sunshine" and "When You Wish upon a Star" were replaced by "This Is My Country" and "Praise the Lord and Pass the Ammunition." Quonset huts sprang up like mushrooms. Twenty-four hours after the blow of Pearl Harbor, Hollywood was mobilizing.

Loyalty and patriotism were words that meant a great deal in 1941, unsullied by later experiences in Korea and Vietnam. Most people associated with the film industry felt that they would do anything in their power to aid the war effort. There was an ingrained hatred of Hitler and all he stood for plus fury at the sneak attack on Hawaii. Entertainers by and large rose to the defense of their country.

Hollywood's attitudes were no different from those of any other American city, but a lot more publicity was attached to the men who marched off to war—and to the ones who stayed behind. A snide remark that made the studio rounds said, "On December 8, 1941,

My wardrobe for the film *Down in Arkansas* consisted largely of overalls.
Despite its title, the movie was made entirely in the Sierras of California.

there were two kinds of men in Hollywood—those looking for enlistment centers and those looking for loopholes."

There were various ways to avoid serving in the armed forces. Studios could obtain "Washington deferments" for favored actors. Film people could get preferential treatment as part of an "essential" industry. There was a lot of persuasive power in the logical reasoning, "If I go, I'll be forgotten."

Among those who marched off with honor were Henry Fonda, Robert Taylor, Clark Gable, Red Skelton, Gene Autry, and Jimmy Stewart. Lew Ayres went to a conscientious-objector camp for his beliefs and then served with distinction in the medical corps.

I was drafted, passed my physical, and was then exempted. I didn't ask for any special deferment. One wife and two children was an automatic exemption in 1942. These were the rules early in the war, plus the fact I was over twenty-eight, which was the upper limit at the time.

I took up home-front duties at the Hollywood Canteen. This effort was sponsored by many trade associations, such as Actors Equity; the Screenwriters Guild; ASCAP; the makeup, hairdresser, and carpenter unions, and the USO. Bette Davis served as president of the canteen. The names of her five vice-presidents read like a Hollywood who's who: Mervyn LeRoy, Mrs. John Ford, John Garfield, J. K. Wallace, and Carroll Hollister.

Mervyn LeRoy was in charge of securing hosts. He approached me with the idea of me being the staff master of ceremonies. I accepted and practically camped at 1451 North Cahuenga—the Hollywood Canteen. We produced short shows and provided refreshments and dances and a place for servicemen to drop in.

It's really true that all the stars gave graciously of their time in this effort. It was not unusual for actors and actresses to drop in to chat with the boys, serve refreshments, and sign autographs. The famous newspaper photos of servicemen dancing with big-name stars weren't publicity shots. A lot of high-priced talent spent a lot of hours at the Hollywood Canteen. Bette Davis wrote nice thank-you letters to everyone who participated. Over a million servicemen visited the Hollywood Canteen. Number one million was Carl Bell, who got a star-studded welcome from Marlene Dietrich, Lana Turner, Deanna Durbin, and Carey Wilson.

World War II pumped new life into the song market. Sentimental songs with a patriotic twist were surefire favorites. Part of this was effective marketing, but the mood of the nation actually was "Don't Sit Under the Apple Tree with Anyone Else but Me." The Andrews Sisters, Maxine, Patti, and La Verne, smashed popularity charts with their bouncing harmonic vocals. They made a hit record of my song "The Trouble with Me Is You."

Radio still ruled as the nation's chief entertainer, though more time was devoted to newscasts. NBC and CBS slugged each other for airwave supremacy as the number of radios in America topped thirty million. William Paley, head of CBS, lured Red Skelton, Amos and Andy, and Burns and Allen away from the rival network. He bought Jack Benny's "Amusement Enterprises" setup for a flat $1.4 million and then moved the whole thing to CBS.

The entertainment business turned to performing for the troops. In 1942 my agent at William Morris called, telling me about a new kind of show for servicemen. It was to be called the Camel Caravan after its cigarette sponsor. They wanted me to go on tour with the new troupe. "Pinky, it would mean a lot of travel and not much salary. But I don't have to tell you how much good it will do."

I took my responsibilities seriously, as a family man, an entertainer, and an American. I hated to be gone from Joanne, daughter, Sylvia, and new son, Tom, but the Camel Caravan seemed like a more meaningful effort than emceeing at the Hollywood Canteen.

I signed on with the R. J. Reynolds Tobacco Company to manage and emcee the Camel Caravan. We made up a cast along the lines of the USO troupes. I performed my own songs. The Sons of the Pioneers did instrumentals and vocals. Vivi Brown, our cancan dancer, was always a huge hit. Marilyn Maxwell was the "socko" girl singer. We had a couple of comedy acts and a supporting cast of four beautiful young ladies who wore short shorts and circulated through the audience distributing free packs of cigarettes.

We did these shows self-contained. The basic stage was a large circus truck with let-down sides and end gate. We could back into

Hollywood Canteen

Affiliated With American Theatre Wing, Inc.

HOLLYWOOD 28, CALIFORNIA

March 29, 1944

Pinky Tomlin
10525 Wilkins
West Los Angeles, Calif.

Dear Pinky Tomlin:

Please accept the gratitude of the
Hollywood Canteen Board of Directors
for your faithfulness in coming to
the Canteen so often and so regularly.

Only we who spend a great deal of our
time here know how very much the service
men appreciate entertainment. I am
certain that your presence at the Canteen
has added a lot to making for pleasant
memories of Hollywood for the boys who
have seen you here.

Please allow us to wish you the very
best of things, and be assured of our
kindest regards.

Sincerely,

Bette Davis

Bette Davis
President

This thank-you letter from Bette Davis was for my work as staff master of
ceremonies at the Hollywood Canteen during World War II.

position, open the sides, and have our arena. The Sons of the Pioneers memorized the musical arrangements for everyone's numbers so that there would be no hassle with music stands in wind or snow.

Although I'd vowed never to go back on the one-night-stand circuit, I found myself doing one-day stands from 1942 to 1944. These stints were every bit as grueling as the band tour. We'd pull up to a parade ground on a military base, unfold our truck, and be in business an hour later. Our troupe took along its own electricians and stage managers. We commonly had five or six thousand men in the audience, often gathering around long before the show began. There has never been a more enthusiastic audience than those troops.

We often did as many as six shows a day. We played supply depots, Army bases, submarine piers, Coast Guard hospitals, Marine Corps barracks, and the Navy net depots as far away as the Aleutian Islands, off Alaska. Several times the commanding officers would tell us our audience was due to be shipped out. The idea of performing for men who were serving us kept the caliber of the Camel Caravan high.

The constant traveling and performing six times a day was a strain. I managed an occasional visit home. Several times my family met me in the San Francisco vicinity. When our show received clearance from the War Department, the travels increased again. When we came across other performing troupes, such as Bob Hope's, we'd join forces and produce a spectacular. The favorites with the men were usually Marilyn Maxwell and the comedy duo Abbott and Costello.

Once I tried to calculate how many miles we traveled and how many men we entertained, but the figures got hopelessly tangled somewhere in the millions. For all its strain, inconvenience, and economic hardship, the wartime tours were some of my most rewarding moments in show business.

Most Americans sacrificed during the war, but performers made economic sacrifices that were directly opposite to the benefits of their nonentertainer counterparts. Wages in civilian defense plants skyrocketed. The earnings of show-business people plummeted. In 1940 the highest wage earner in the United States was Gary Cooper, with an income of $482,821. He beat out the presidents of IBM, Lever Brothers, and General Motors. The second-highest-paid actor that year was James Cagney, with an income of $368,333. I wasn't in that economic bracket by any means, but retiring from films and band-leading cost me plenty. Heading the Camel Caravan cost me about $100,000 the first year and around $35,000 a year for the duration. My salary from R. J. Reynolds was only a token sum, nowhere near enough to cover out-of-pocket expenses or to maintain my family. Gene Autry once quipped that he took a $950,000 pay cut to serve in the armed forces. He wasn't alone in finding that wartime meant economic sacrifice.

One of the ways I made ends meet during the war was to sell off some real estate I'd purchased in 1935. Back then a new ranch complex had opened in the Northridge area. Quite a few show-business people bought acreages and then built ranch houses. Some of the bungalows in the hills belonged to Robert Taylor, Barbara Stanwyck, Carole Lombard, Clark Gable, and Zeppo Marx.

I bought eleven and a half acres in the Northridge development with the idea of using it as a weekend retreat. My neighbor over the hill was Chester Lauck, who played Lum on the "Lum and Abner" radio show. When I purchased the land in 1935 it cost me $1,000 an acre. When I checked the area in 1973, I found that prices were up to $65,000 an acre, but I had to sell my holdings before the great boom in southern California real estate. I helped cover my wartime expenses by selling out for $1,500 an acre.

I lost so much money doing the Camel Caravan that I finally went to the William Morris Agency and told them that I either had to quit or find a way to be reimbursed. "Replace me or raise my salary," I said, putting my cards on the table.

"Stay with the show for now," they countered, "Then we'll make sure your career booms after the war."

After some difficult haggling, we reached a compromise. They would put a bit more money in the pot for now. When the war ended, they'd set me up on the personal-appearance-tour circuit at a guaranteed $2,000 a week. The salary sounded good, but I wondered what they had in mind for the length of the tour.

Johnny Hyde figured, "We could get you twenty weeks of bookings with no trouble. That should help restore your financial health."

Twenty weeks back on the road—was that all I was going to have to look forward to after victory? Actually it was in the back of my mind to avoid going back into the entertainment world altogether.

I had a young family and a faithful wife who had spent the war years as abandoned as if I'd been overseas. It was time to plan for a future that would let me live at home. But the best offer I had in sight was the agency's twenty weeks at $2,000 a week. "All right, let's set it up," I told them. "But I want some say in planning the itinerary."

"Fine," said Johnny Hyde. "Where do you want to play?"

To his amazement, I listed such out-of-the-way places such as Cheyenne, Wyoming; Billings, Montana; and Midland, Texas. "And I want a firm date in Tulsa, Oklahoma, too. Yeah, and put Odessa on the tour."

"Odessa? Where's that?"

"Texas." I didn't add, "right in the middle of the oil industry," but that's what I was thinking. I had a geology minor from a university with an international reputation in petroleum exploration. My son's godfather, Allen Calvert, was a leading figure in the national oil industry. My longtime friend Eddie Chiles, of the Western Company of North America, had offered aid if I ever wanted to dabble in the oil patch. I decided that the time had come to call on these resources. My first step was to make sure my postwar tour took me to towns where I could renew friendships and make contacts.

The war finally came to an end in 1945. Emotions overflowed—and Hollywood's emotions overflowed, too, as it tried to cope with a new kind of audience. During the war few pictures had failed to show a profit. It seemed that anyone with a couple of hours to spare had popped into a movie theater. Studio and theater income topped $1 billion for the first time in 1943.

In 1946 it became apparent that America was demobilizing more than the arsenal of democracy. The studios faced a mass exit of actors, directors, and technicians who decided to remain civilians, far, far away from Hollywood.

When price controls were finally lifted on gasoline, food, and rent, costs zoomed. Salaries for performers skyrocketed too. A new breed of high-powered agents took over neogitiations, often delegating half-million-dollar salaries and percentages of the gross. A new gadget, television, came on the scene, but most industry people scoffed at it. A common remark was, "Who'd sit around staring at a box?"

The movie men fought postwar inflation by raising ticket prices. *The Best Years of Our Lives* was sent out as a road-show attraction with a hefty $3.50-a-seat cost. The movie eventually returned $10 million, but the cost-price spiral was entrenched by then.

The federal government dealt the studios a crushing blow by filing antitrust suits to separate the production facilities from their commercial theaters. RKO and Paramount caved in and sold off their movie houses. MGM, Twentieth Century Fox, and Warner Brothers filed countersuits. The battle took five years and cost millions of dollars with the same result. The last of the chains were sold.

Another important postwar blow to Hollywood economics was the income tax. The high-dollar deals were suddenly not so tempting. A role that paid $100,000 meant $85,000 for Uncle Sam and only $15,000 for the actor. Tax shelters became the big thing. "Form a corporation" became Hollywood's watchword. Performers decided not to sit around and let their salary go for taxes. They turned to making films, producing records, promoting concerts, dealing in real estate, and ranching.

I turned to oil. The transition period after the war saw me trying to cover all bases. I went before the cameras in the postwar era for *The Story of Will Rogers* and *Here Comes Elmer*. I played out my concert dates in accordance with my William Morris Agency agreement. I also laid the groundwork for my new venture, Pinky Tomlin Oil Properties.

During my crosscountry headliner tour of 1946–47, I held meetings with old oil-field acquaintances at the Park Lane Hotel in Denver, the Mayo in Tulsa, and the Baker in Dallas. Part of my agreement with William Morris was that they would double the publicity and marquee space in each large city. Most of my play dates sold out in advance, with many of my friends in the audience. In the reunions after the show I sought and received a lot of valuable advice about my new oil venture. My friend Eddie Chiles handed me a blank check and said, "Fill it in for whatever you need to get started."

I didn't need the blank check, but I did have to have loans to get going. I saved all I could from my concert tour, liquidated some property holdings, and consolidated all my spare cash. I knew that it would take several years to make a small independent oil-and-gas-lease company flourish. I remembered my overnight success in song-writing when I'd gone to California in 1934 and played the Biltmore Bowl. I wasn't so optimistic about Pinky Tomlin Oil Properties. I knew that some hard work would be involved; there would not be another overnight bonanza.

Good advice and financial backing tided me over this getting-started period. Earl Sullins, a friend and former football coach from Ponca City, Oklahoma, participated in some of my ventures. He was inducted into the National High School Hall of Fame for his football prowess. I'd say he deserves a spot in my hall of fame for good friends, too. The owners of the Oil Capitol Corporation of Tulsa, Garth Caylor and Chuck March, provided backing. Bill Gothard and Ron Stanhope, from Montana, joined me in some ventures. People like Fred Dilts, from Douglas, Wyoming, helped me learn the oil business from the bottom of the sump pit to the top of the derrick.

Interestingly, I found that promoting an oil deal was not much different from promoting a song. In both worlds it's best to show an honest face, be enthusiastic, and tend to your business absolutely straight.

News of my new oil-and-gas-lease company spread throughout the entertainment industry. Bob Taylor made it a point to find my new office and pay me a visit. Tactfully he indicated that he wanted to help me out. "I don't know anything about the oil business, Pinky, but if you're involved, count me in."

I felt we'd come full circle. A decade before, he'd been the struggling young actor and I'd been the established name. Remembering back to our good times on *Times Square Lady* made me doubly appreciative of his offers of help now. Taylor's faith in me went beyond merely putting his own money into the speculative world of oil exploration. He introduced me to his financial adviser, A. Morgan Maree. Bob told Maree simply, "Find out about Pinky's projects, and then include me in any and all of them."

A. Morgan Maree and Associates represented many of Hollywood's wealthiest stars. Many of the actors and actresses were in the postwar 90 percent tax bracket. Any reasonable investment was an assistance to them in maintaining their finances. Maree liked the plans I had for my company and the knowledge I had to back them up. He sent me clients, including Barbara Stanwyck, Humphrey Bogart, Joseph Cotten, Dick Powell, Dennis Morgan, and Eve Arden. I knew that all this backing came about because of my old friend Robert Taylor.

In the early years of my company I was not so well established that I could turn down chances to perform. I filmed *Here Comes Elmer* with Al Pearce, Morey Amsterdam, Tizzy Lish, and Dale Evans. In that variety film I sang "Don't Be Afraid to Tell Your Mother," which I had written and which was Al Pearce's favorite.

In 1951 I had a part in the Warner Brothers' movie *The Story of Will Rogers*. Will Rogers, Jr., played the part of his father with Jane Wyman costarring. I sang Will's favorite song, "Home on the Range," and did a square-dance call. The scene was done right, featuring the time when Oklahoma gained entrance to the Union as a state.

This film was premiered at Claremore, Oklahoma, near Will's hometown, Oologah. Will Rogers, Jr., was to be guest of honor. He had spent very little time in Oklahoma and felt unsure about doing the promotion. He asked me to come along as a fellow Oklahoman. "Come with me," he drawled, sounding just like his dad. "We'll have a fine time, and you can keep me squared away."

It sounded like a wonderful trip—especially since Warner Brothers was picking up the tab. I joined the entourage as master of ceremonies. We had a big party at the Will Rogers Hotel in Claremore the night before the main festivities. Will Rogers, Jr., and his sister, Mary Rogers, headed the dignitary list. Jane Wyman, my wife and I, and about twenty-five other California representatives were present. We were joined by public officials, a few national officeholders, many of my wife's relatives, and our Oklahoma friends. The next day Will, Jr., Mary Rogers, Jane Wyman, Joanne, and I all rode on horseback in a parade. A barbecue and rodeo followed. The premiere of the movie was held that evening and was a great success.

Besides doing occasional movies, I also went on band and concert tours through the later forties. The same tough conditions of travel

Will Rogers, Jr., Mary Rogers, and I ride in the parade at Claremore, Oklahoma, during premiere festivities for the 1952 film *The Story of Will Rogers*.

and arrangements existed as before. Now I was attempting to spread myself even thinner with a business to run. Something had to give. It finally did, courtesy of my son, Tom. He made some amateur booking arrangements on my behalf that prompted me to move fulltime into business and give up touring entirely.

I arrived home from a two-week singing engagement in Omaha, Nebraska. As usual, I hit the house tired, wanting nothing more than a hot shower and some sleep. Tom gave me a hug and said, "I have to talk to you, Daddy."

"Not now."

His mouth began trembling, and tears welled up in his eyes. I realized that something big was troubling him. Sitting down, I held him, wondering when the last time was that I'd had any time for my family. "What's wrong, son?"

"While you were gone—say, where were you this time?"

"Nebraska," I said wearily, disturbed that neither my family nor I could keep track of my travels. This fast, blurred life wasn't doing any of us any good. "What happened while I was gone?"

"Mama was crying."

I worried that my wife had been ill or perhaps there'd been an accident.

Tom said, "When I asked her what was wrong, she said that it was her birthday and she was lonesome."

I felt doubly bad. It was lousy to forget a birthday, but even worse, I seemed to be harming both my wife and children with my absences. Spontaneously I made my son a promise. "I'll be around for Mama's next birthday—and yours and Sylvia's too."

He seemed a bit consoled. "I have something else to tell you. I signed up to play Little League baseball at the park today."

"That's great. I know you'll like baseball."

"We had tryouts, and I made the team."

Congratulations were definitely in order. I bragged on my son, but he kept frowning. What was the matter now? "Aren't you glad, Tom?"

"Well, I told them you used to be a pitcher on a college baseball team."

"That's true—nothing to feel bad about."

"But I told them you were such a good baseball player that you'd be our team manager."

That did it. From that moment on, I knew where to concentrate my energies. My life was going to focus on our home in Brentwood, California, and not somewhere out in the bright lights of America's theaters.

It's an anticlimax to say that for the next few years I was involved deeply in the youth baseball program. Joanne was president of women's auxiliary for the league. We sold hot dogs and soda pop to finance the team's new uniforms. One of my proudest days was when I was listed as a charter member of the Little League organization of Los Angeles.

24

Where's Hollywood?

When television came of age, everything in Hollywood changed, including the scenery. Twentieth Century's back lot now sprouted high-rise buildings. Lucy and Desi split up, but not before they'd created the giant Desilu Productions out of the shambles of RKO. Metro-Goldwyn-Mayer held a series of auctions in which they sold off talent, directors, managers, and props. Universal had more shakeups than California had earthquakes.

Television, antitrust rulings, taxes, and foreign investments all took their toll on Hollywood. Foreign countries began freezing film assets. When moviemakers couldn't bring their sterling, francs, or lire home from overseas, they moved the production companies to meet the money. By the mid-1950s the movie capital looked like a ghost town.

The mecca for live performance shifted slightly eastward to Las Vegas. Today it is nearly the only place to see show business "in person." Some entertainers credit the mass exodus to Vegas showrooms as being the work of one man, Jack Entratter. He moved from New York's Copacabana to the new Las Vegas Sands in 1952, bringing west some advanced ideas about booking procedures. His theory was to hire big names at big salaries. There's no doubt about the effectiveness of big money. Soon Entratter had a rivalry going with booker Frank Sennes at the Desert Inn. In 1953, Bill Miller thought up the idea of adding entertainment in the lounge at the Sahara. He hired my old friend Louis Prima to do five shows a night at $3,500 a week.

Las Vegas glimmered like a city with streets of gold at a time when

185

stars were still shrugging off television and scoffing at commercials. When Las Vegas began billing itself as the "showplace of the world," no one was left in Hollywood to object. In fact, everyone was busy signing on with the big hotels along the Strip.

I played Vegas several times. My original performance was at the El Rancho. That lovely hotel had copied the architecture of a New Mexico ranch belonging to independent theater owner R. E. Griffith. Mr. Griffith, a competitive Oklahoman, was reasonably angry about the use of his ranch's architecture. He set out to build something bigger and better across the street from the El Rancho.

When Griffith finished the Last Frontier Hotel, he asked me to open the place with a western-style show. I headlined a "no-holds-barred" entertainment calculated to put the competition across the street in their place. Later the El Rancho burned under suspicious circumstances. The Last Frontier Hotel is now billed as the New Frontier.

Las Vegas has recently reached some new frontiers in performer's contracts too. Barbra Streisand's $500,000 a week and Johnny Carson's multimillion-dollar deals barely rate headlines in *Variety*. No one blinked twice when Caesar's Palace sold for $6 million in 1970.

People go to Vegas to gamble, to see the showgirls, and to watch the headliners. The town stays busy year round. Little sister Reno is now making it to the big-time ranks, but it hasn't hurt the original star at all.

Meanwhile, back at the Hollywood ranch, celluloid has tried to perk up the box office with unclothed bodies and dirty words. The latest catch words in the industry are "go-go" and "disco." Tomorrow it will be something new as the film studios play catch-up in a losing battle. The new trends to made-for-television movies and home-box-office systems threaten all the studios, from the conglomerates to independents.

Recently some friends and I were discussing the unhappy state of film art. We ended up writing a new song, "Where's Hollywood?" The words are by Vic Knight and me with music by Harry Freiberg and Don Shaw:

186

Hollywood, Where's Hollywood?
Has the place disappeared for good?
They sell you a map to a movie star's home,
But where is that star now? Living in Rome!

Hollywood, Where's Hollywood?
Have they changed it around, but good?
An old actor said, he believes beyond doubt
The whole town has made such a big turnabout
That the footprints at Grauman's Chinese just walked out!
Where's Hollywood today?

Hollywood, Where's Hollywood?
Where's the glamour for which it stood?
Where are all the stars that the city now lacks?
They're in a museum made out of wax!

Hollywood, Where's Hollywood?
Has the place disappeared for good?
The Garbos and Gables all said their farewells
The new Shirley Temples are all Jezebels,
And the famous back lots are now high rise hotels.
Where's Hollywood today?

© *TNT Music*, 1976

It should be apparent that I'm still interested in popular music. I wrote my first song, "Object," in 1933. "Where's Hollywood?" and "Old Fashioned Christmas" were composed in 1976, and I've had a few ideas lately I mean to put on paper.

Today's song market is glutted. It puts almost insurmountable obstacles in the path of new talent. How are our Perry Comos, Peggy Lees, and Frankie Laines of the future to be heard as soloists? Too many of today's performers front with nine guitars and a light show and cover their lack of talent with background singers and electronic mixers.

Those who have performed solo on empty stages know that "in person" is a true test of what talent you have to offer. I identify strongly with individual performers. In the music world my favorites are Perry Como for ballads, Robert Merrill for opera, Ella Fitzgerald for all-around vocals, and Karen Carpenter for female ballads. Beverly Sills tops the list for classics. In other specialties I'd say Gene Kelly, Fred Astaire, and Eleanor Powell rate as all-time dance champs. Spencer Tracy and Katharine Hepburn were my personal favorites on the screen.

I'm proud of the fraternal spirit that exists among show-business people. Besides being profoundly dedicated to their profession, most entertainers are generous and good-natured. The outer layer of show business is sometimes glamourized to be "phony as it can be," but the people at the core should be given credit for their interest and humanity in charitable good works. Everyone knows of Jerry Lewis and his telethons for muscular dystrophy, but there are many similar, unpublicized efforts by entertainers. Nowadays it's rare to find a gathering of superstars unless the reason is a charity function. At these get-togethers they seek each other out, give a pat on the back, a friendly smile, and a handshake of encouragement. This aspect of show business is one I'm proud to be part of.

In 1980 I enjoyed serving as master of ceremonies and performer at the annual Valentine Ball sponsored by the Beverly Hills Chamber of Commerce. The honoree for the year was the talented singer Ella Fitzgerald. In making preparations for the event, she reminded me that back in 1935, when she auditioned at the Apollo Theatre in New York, she used "The Object of My Affection" as her tryout number. It was delightful to honor this woman whose voice has inspired and delighted millions.

My bit consisted of singing three songs—the big one was "The Object of My Affection"—which led into the presentation of the inimitable and unbeatable Ella. It was like an opening night for me and as thrilling as years before when I received many such standing ovations. As I walked off, Ella walked on with a smile and a pat on my back as we passed each other.

I had the extreme pleasure of sitting back in the audience and letting her do the work. Mike Douglas of TV fame interviewed her, and

Ella Fitzgerald and I with former Oklahoman Jimmy Baker of ABC TV at the 1980 Beverly Hills Chamber of Commerce Valentine Ball, at which Ella received the Will Rogers Memorial Award.

Singing at the Valentine Ball in 1980.

she told the story of how she got started. She was just a kid who had entered an amateur contest held at the Apollo Theater in Harlem in New York City. She was to do a dance to the tune of "The Object of My Affection." When it was her turn to go on stage, she turned to her mother, who was standing in the wings with her, and said, "I can't do it, my legs are jellified." Her mother shoved her forward and said firmly, "Sing it." Then, as she described it, "Wanting and needing to win this contest, I sang my heart out. When I got to the part of the lyric 'can change my complexion from white to rosy red,' I felt the compulsion to improvise and sang, 'from brown to rosy red' instead. This change broke up the place. I won the contest hands down. I might add, if it hadn't been for ol' Pinky, all of this mess would not have started for me in the first place." She looked at me and smiled. I said, "Thank you for singing it, Ella." She replied, "Thank you, Pinky, for writing it."

The Valentine Ball also honors an outstanding citizen of Beverly Hills. Jimmy McHugh, author of "Sunny Side of the Street" and other great hits, and I were members of the entertainment committee for the ball one year. We devised the award, known as the Will Rogers Memorial Award, won by Ella Fitzgerald in 1980. Some of the past recipients of the award have been Jack Benny, Dinah Shore, Art Linkletter, and George Jessel.

The people to whom I was closest in show business were people you'd be proud to know in any profession. Among my favorite individuals were Robert Taylor, Bing Crosby, George Jessel, George Burns, Ricardo Montalban, Jane Wyman, Gene Kelly, Fred Astaire, Bob Hope, and Jerry Lewis. When I talk about favorite bandleaders, I mean the people behind the batons and not their organization's musical quality. Some of the finest people I've known have been Freddie Martin, Harry James, Guy Lombardo, Jimmy Grier, Louis Armstrong, Louis Prima, Jimmy Dorsey, and Les Brown.

On the subject of modern music I have mixed emotions. Louis Armstrong once called bop a "modern malice." I'm not certain rock 'n' roll has done our eardrums any favors. We now have a situation in which beat dominates melody and electronics dominate everything. In the old days, when we tuned our instruments, we'd smile and say,

"Man, that's close enough for jazz!" Now we're producing a kind of music that uses tapes, tracks, and mixes and has no need for instruments.

It's hard to hum along with the melody when records are now made on magentic tape that carries up to twenty-four tracks or more. You can record a different sound effect on every channel, then merge the noises of synthesizers, transistors, computers, and potentiometers into a completely new music.

My chief quarrel with electric gadgets is the trouble caused with copyright and performance rules. The jukebox did entertainers more harm than good, in my opinion. Most jukebox owners were given records free as demonstrators. They then collected all those nickels, dimes, and quarters while the performer got nothing. I recall a huge outdoor ballroom in San Antonio, Texas, that never used live music. They'd roll a stereo onto the floor and finance their entire operation free. ASCAP tries to remedy this kind of situation, but performers and composers have lost millions of dollars over the years through such musical subversion.

My own love for music has lasted me over half a century. It has fed me, bankrolled me, given me a measure of independence, and provided me with untold pleasure. I've written it, danced to it, listened to it, criticized it, defended it, and enjoyed it. I even wrote a poem about it:

> To soothe the breast of savage man
> Music hath the charm
> But rock and roll, so I am told
> Is causing much alarm.
> There are no rules for musical fools,
> They sing and write galore
> But it got man's goat
> When someone wrote,
> It ain't gonna rain no more.
>
> But songs have changed a lot since then
> To enhance this form of art.

192

To some you only pat your foot
But others touch your heart.
I tip my hat to Johnny Mercer, Cole Porter, and the rest
who wrote the words and music to our country's very best.

In my years of ups and downs and ins and outs through the musical world, I've been aided by many people. One of the most influential and knowledgeable women in music publishing circles is Mrs. S. H. ("Bonnie") Bourne, owner and head of Bourne Music Company in New York City. This firm was originally the Irving Berlin Company, which bought my first song. Bourne bought all the songs and copyrights except those of Irving Berlin. Bourne is a huge organization and one of the few independents left in the business. Bonnie Bourne has brought a lot of prestige, finesse, and graciousness to a business that is known for being hard-nosed. She is truly a great lady. As musicians put it, "She's somethin' else."

The years have played a lot of musical tricks on me, but the most amazing thing is that time has proved that my first song was my best. Royalties from "The Object of My Affection" strill trickle in sort of like stock dividends. It's really true that when records spin they're spinning music into gold. Lately I collected small amounts of "Object"'s use in such diverse productions as "One Day at a Time" on television, *Paper Moon* in movie theaters, and the series "This Gun for Hire" in reruns.

My last royalty sheet showed that "Object" and several others of my songs are still popular in such places as Norway, Australia, Holland, Japan, Denmark, South Africa, England, Germany, and Sweden. In France, "L'Objet de mon affection" remains a perennial favorite.

It's wonderful having this little nest egg of royalty developed from an inspiration of fifty years ago. I feel I have also been lucky in being able to make the transition from performer to private life. It was important to find something to do independent of image, pink hair, sentimental music, and travel. I remain active in the oil-and-gas-lease business, and I'd be the first to say that putting a deal together in the oil patch is every bit as exciting as show business.

I have made many good friends in the petroleum industry. Maxine Amick, in Billings, Montana, has always been helpful in acquiring leases in the Rocky Mountain area. Betty Tuttle, in Cheyenne, Wyoming, is one of the country's most knowledgeable people about state and federal land leasing in the area. Down in Longview, Texas, Marshall Hayes III has proved a good friend and a smart man in the shallow field plays.

My friend of longest standing in the drilling business is Eddie Chiles. We renew contact whenever he's on the West Coast or I'm in Fort Worth, Texas. On a visit I made to Fort Worth to do some geologic research, I called Eddie's corporate headquarters. We had dinner at his home, followed by a lot of college-days reminiscing. After supper, in the den, I noticed a guitar leaning against the fireplace. Coincidence? I picked it up and started strumming. Eddie considered that a cue to invite everyone on the premises in for a song fest. I begged off after two hours, having sung and played nearly every song I ever wrote or learned.

Eddie advised me about the research I'd been doing. It concerned an area near Waco, Texas. He looked at the maps and my findings and then said: "Take it. Drill it. Produce it and sell it. Whatever you need, anything at all, you can get right here, no strings attached." Then he threw back his head and laughed, adding, "except the strings on that guitar that I sneaked into the den last night."

25

Full Circle

Timing is one of the most important aspects in any career. I've experienced more good timing than bad in both my show-business and oil professions, but there have been problems. I find it ironic that oil was discovered near Durant about the time that I entered the oil-and-gas-leasing industry. Offshore wells ring the eastern edges of Lake Texoma, about twenty miles from my hometown. As a kid growing up in Bryan County, I never paid any attention to oil. After I moved to California and my parents had died, my brothers and I still owned a 320-acre farm in Blue River bottom. Its only value, as far as we knew, was in the land. The price of land in the thirties wasn't very much. We sold out for fifteen dollars an acre. In 1950, Standard Oil paid the new owners forty dollars an acre just to look for oil. Nothing was discovered, but that's a case where my timing was certainly poor.

Musically and privately, I've managed to have good timing. I still like to sing. I'm still married to my original sweetheart after forty-two years.

One nice experience was being recognized musically at Oklahoma University in the mid-sixties. I was invited to return to a football game as guest of honor and to perform with the band at halftime. Leonard Haug, band director, featured my songs in the presentation. Haug and I went back a long way, all the way to the thirties, when he'd been OU bandmaster and I'd been leading the campus Boomer Band.

My wife and two children accompanied me for this October trip.

Joanne and Pinky Tomlin in 1976.

There was a parade with a special car, and I served as judge of the homecoming decorations. For two days before the halftime show, I rehearsed with the university band, known as "The Pride of Oklahoma."

On Saturday it was a delight to be back in Owen Stadium among sixty thousand fans. The halftime program opened with my composition, "In Ole Oklahoma." I climbed onto a pedestal and sang three songs, using a four-speaker public-address system. For the occasion we picked the snappy numbers "What's the Reason I'm Not Pleasin' You?" and "The Love Bug Will Bite You If You Don't Watch Out." I closed with the song everyone recognized, "The Object of My Affection." The ovation that followed ranks as one of the biggest thrills in my life.

My appearance with the OU band seemed a nice way to say thank-you to my many Oklahoma and college friends. I've encountered them all across America, as performers and musicians, in all areas of show business and petroleum exploration. Invariably Oklahomans have proved friendly and helpful. One of my many contacts, Jimmie Baker, attended school at Tulsa University and Oklahoma State University. He is now program director for ABC-TV.

Some California residents who have helped me include physicians Samuel P. Benbrook, Harley Gunderson, and chemosurgeon Theodore Tromovitch. Attorneys Gordon Levoy and Ralph Frank and real-estate broker Michael Kopcha have been knowledgeable in their fields, and I have been helped in contract matters by Keith Hesselbarth at the Security Pacific Bank in Beverly Hills.

Most of all, I've been aided by enthusiastic audiences in every part of America. I've stuck around through four wars, the Great Depression, several recessions both economic and personal, and worldwide changes in musical taste, and yet I feel I still have something to offer. Early on I acquired a knack for rolling with the punches. With that ability, coupled with a fierce desire to succeed, I've been able to adjust to many changes in the last half century.

I find that people endowed with creativity almost always find themselves burdened with sensitivity. I've tried to recognize that trait in my own personality and compensate for disappointments that have come my way. The lyrics about "people needing people" work beautifully as a song, but in real life there have been some people I could have done without. In this book I've tried to keep the spotlight on folks who were helpful. I've ignored those who provided me with my share of hurts, slights, or harms. Hedda Hopper often insisted that movie people had to be born show-offs. Maybe, but I realize that show-business personalities often have a lot of personal drive. Sometimes that energy boomerangs, sending them into situations that don't work out. As for the people who have put stumbling blocks in my path or disappointed me on a personal level, I'll let silence speak in place of rebuttal.

Perhaps in my next life I'll be able to satisfy all my critics. If I had the chance, I'd like to come back as a multitalented person. I'd enjoy having the true grit of a John Wayne, the intellectual prowess of a William Buckley, and the political wisdom a lot of actors think they have. I'd like to be as cute and physical as Burt Reynolds and have the energy and ability to rouse an audience the way Dinah Shore can. What a breeze that life would be! Actually, there are some things I'd keep from this go-round. I'd hope to retain my belief that few things are impossible and that it's never too late to try.

Over the years I came to believe that a person needed few things in life. There are only three essentials: work to do, someone to love, and something to hope for.

In my life I've worked hard, being self-sufficient since I was twelve. My first love was an enduring one. Our son Tom and daughter Sylvia are grown. We have four grandchildren: Bob and Ann Riley and Mike and Jon Tomlin. Certainly I don't need to make any further comments on my having someone to love.

Finally, I hope for many things. Regardless of how long a life-span may run, the "something to hope for" seems paramount in keeping you active, healthy, and happy. This hoping has allowed me to do many things that would logically have been beyond the reach of a southeastern-Oklahoma kid. Fortunately I lived in an era when kindness, good manners, and devotion to family were respected traits.

Along my way I've never been afraid to aim for the stars. Luckily, a lot of stardust graced my travels. Johnny Lange, a fellow ASCAP

Our grandchildren are Bob and Ann Riley and Mike and Jon Tomlin.

composer, paid me a nice compliment when he said, "It wasn't all vinegar that came from those grapes of wrath in Oklahoma. I'd call Pinky fine wine!"

A comment like that sounds mellow indeed. I'm grateful that my voice remains mellow, too. I can perform when called on to do a charity benefit. Along with a clear voice, I put a lot of time and effort into any performance I give. Frankie Laine once insisted that I had a voice "you can hug." I think he was referring to my straightforward tonality that keeps the sound warm and honest. I never use musical tricks that take attention away from the melody. As we say in the trade, "It's hard to beat an old swinger." I might add, "Especially if he knows what he's doing."

I had the chance to prove that I still know my business in 1976, when the Hathaway House for Children held a fund-raising benefit at the Hollywood Biltmore. The Hathaway House facilities had burned during the great canyon fire that had swept Malibu and Little Tujunga

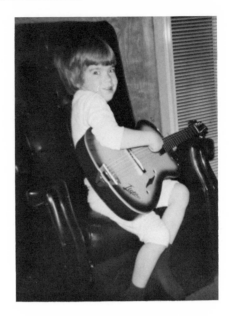

Grandson Mike Tomlin tries
out my guitar.

Canyon in 1975. The evening at the Biltmore Bowl was to be a dinner
dance and show to support the rebuilding efforts. The orchestra for
the occasion was Freddie Martin's, the vocal group was the Moder-
naires, and the entertainer was me.

When my wife and I walked into the Biltmore Bowl that night, it
had been forty-two years since I'd first performed on the stage. It gave
me a sense of déjà vu to remember how I'd nervously waited my
chance with Jimmy Grier's orchestra, sung "The Object of My Affection," and won the audience. You'd think that in the next forty-two
years I would have acquired a certain amount of confidence, but I was
as excited in 1976 as if I'd just arrived from Oklahoma with one blue
suit and a guitar.

Joanne looked around the packed house and pointed out how many of our good friends had come for the special evening. "And there's lots of younger people, kids in their twenties and thirties. That really adds to the occasion."

"This will be like a captive audience," I mused, "So many of these folks have heard me over the years."

Believe me, that performance was no off-the-cuff spot. I'd had Freddie Martin's arranger, Sid Appleman, do all-fresh musical arrangements so that I could fit my voice to the orchestra's instrumentation. I was determined to look and sound classy—even if I couldn't roll back the clock forty-two years.

Freddie Martin has never given anyone a nicer introduction than he gave me that night. He told the audience, "Here's a man still active in the oil business, in civic affairs, and, fortunately for us, in the music world." Freddie went on to tell how I'd met my first big-time professional success right in that same room. He said, "Pinky came from Oklahoma and right on this same floor and in this same spot he sang for the first time the song that he'd written and that we are all still humming and that my band is still playing after all these years."

Freddie Martin added a few other flowery phrases, and the response was enthusiastic. Then it was my turn. I came out hoping I remembered all the little tricks, such as getting up close to the audience, maintaining eye contact, and closing with a smash.

During the show I again had the sense of having lived through all this before. It seemed I'd come full circle in life, returning to the Biltmore Bowl to sing the same songs to many of the same people. I even told the audience, "I feel I've returned to the scene of the crime."

My show was well received, all the way from "Ragtime Cowboy Joe" to the inevitable "The Object of My Affection." Afterwards it seemed that everyone in the room came by to shake hands and pat me on the back.

I relaxed, thinking again of the changes in the last forty-two years. This time I wore a tux instead of my old blue suit. I had a hairpiece now to fill in the gaps in my pink hair. One thing didn't change: the exhilaration of performing left me wringing wet.

Later in the evening, after the show, Joanne and I danced by the

Joanne and I arrive at a charity benefit.

bandstand. Good friend Freddie Martin leaned down and kissed me on the foreheard. "You were a smash, you s.o.b.!" Then he handed me the baton to conduct the orchestra and danced away with my wife. Another full-cricle experience—here I was leading a band in the Biltmore Bowl where I'd opened with the Pinky Tomlin Orchestra in 1939.

When we were home that night getting ready for bed, I told Joanne about my strange sensation of having arrived back where I'd started. "If I don't wake up in the morning," I said with a feeling of humility, "let's just say I'm mighty grateful."

Pinky Tomlin

Songs by Pinky Tomlin

Title	Date
"The Object of My Affection"	1934
"What's the Reason I'm Not Pleasin' You?"	1935
"Don't Be Afraid to Tell Your Mother"	1935
"That's What You Think"	1935
"Sweet"	1935
"The Trouble with Me Is You"	1936
"Sittin' on the Edge of My Chair"	1937
"I'm Just a Country Boy at Heart"	1937
"I Told Santa Claus to Bring Me You"	1937
"The Love Bug Will Bite You If You Don't Watch Out"	1937
"In Ole Oklahoma"	1938
"Lost and Found"	1938
"Let's Us Get Together"	1938
"What Are You Doin' Tonight?"	1938
"My, My, Ain't That Somethin'!"	1939
"If It Wasn't for the Moon"	1939
"Love Is All"	1940
"In the Army, in the Navy, in the Marines"	1943
"The Laundromat Song"	1949
"I'm the Worryin' Kind"	1964
"Old Fashioned Christmas"	1976
"Where's Hollywood?"	1976

Films

starring Pinky Tomlin

Title	Studio	Release Date
Times Square Lady	MGM	1935
King Solomon of Broadway	Universal	1935
Smart Girl	Walter Wanger Productions	1935
Paddy O'Day	Twentieth Century-Fox	1936
Don't Get Personal	Universal	1936
Sing While You're Able	Maurice Conn Productions	1937
Thanks for Listenin'	Maurice Conn Productions	1937
With Love and Kisses	Maurice Conn Productions	1937
Down in Arkansas	Republic Pictures	1938
Swing It, Professor	Maurice Conn Productions	1938
Music America Likes	Paramount	1939
Tickled Pinky	Universal	1939
The Pinky Tomlin Orchestra	Universal	1939
The Story of Will Rogers	Warner Brothers	1952

Index

209